Miss Willadene's Fav.'s

A Traditional Southern Cookbook

by

Deborah and Willadene Odom

authorHOUSE®

AuthorHouse™
1663 Liberty Drive, Suite 200
Bloomington, IN 47403
www.authorhouse.com
Phone: 1-800-839-8640

© *2007 Deborah and Willadene Odom. All rights reserved.*

No part of this book may be reproduced, stored in a retrieval system, or transmitted by any means without the written permission of the author.

First published by AuthorHouse 12/18/2007

ISBN: 978-1-4343-1184-9 (sc)
ISBN: 978-1-4343-1183-2 (hc)

Library of Congress Control Number: 2007903513

Printed in the United States of America
Bloomington, Indiana

This book is printed on acid-free paper.

Dedicated to my loving mother, Willadene, and to my supportive brother, David.

Table of Contents

INTRODUCTION ... 1

APPETIZERS & BEVERAGES
- A Party Time Mix ... 7
- Beat the Clock Shake ... 8
- Best Ever Roasted Garlic Butter ... 9
- Cheese Straws ... 10
- Cheese Whip a la Roquefort ... 11
- Chicken Hors D'oeuvre ... 12
- Chicken in Pastry ... 13
- Cream Cheese Spread ... 14
- Exotic Cream Cheese Dip ... 14
- FBI Frozen Thumbprints ... 15
- Gingerale Fruit Punch ... 17
- Green Avocado Dip ... 17
- Party Cheese Ball ... 18
- Pastry Tomato Pizza ... 19
- Pineapple Lemonade ... 20
- Quick Baked Tortilla Chili Dip ... 20
- Uncle Bob's Pimento Cheese Spread ... 21
- Vicky's Punch ... 22
- Whole Roasted Garlic ... 22

SOUPS & SALADS
- A Bouquet Garni ... 27
- Antipasto Salad ... 28
- Avocado Cream Salad Dressing ... 29
- Black Cherry Congealed Salad ... 30
- Blue Cheese Salad Dressing ... 31
- Broccoli Salad ... 32
- Chicken Salad ... 33
- Company Field Green Salad & Dressing ... 34
- Compliment Peach Salad ... 35
- Easy Summer Salad ... 36
- Fight The Cold Chicken And Vegetable Soup ... 37

Four Ingredient Basic Salad Dressing	38
Ham Salad	38
Million Dollar Salad	39
Mothers Five Star Corn Bread Salad	40
Ole' Taco Fiesta Soup	41
Perfect Cole Slaw	42
Pistachio Salad Delight	43
Ranch Dressing in a Pinch	43
Shrimp Salad	44
Sweet Macaroni Salad	45
Thousand Island Salad Dressing	45
Tuna Salad In Its Edible Bowl	46
Whipped Cream Dressing	47

MAIN DISHES

How To Preserve a Husband	52
1-2-3- Chicken and Rice Bake	53
Baked Chicken Breast	54
Baked Pasta with Sausage	55
Baked Red Snapper	56
Baked Salmon Cheese	57
Beef in a Skillet	58
Barbecued Chicken in a Bag	59
Beef Stroganoff	60
Best Chicken & Dumplings	61
Broiled Flounder	62
Chicken & Dumplings # 2	63
Chicken and Rice Bake	64
Chicken Croissant	64
Good Neighbor Casserole	65
Chicken in a Bottle	66
Chicken Mushroom Pie	67
Chicken Parmesan	68
Chicken Pie	69
Chicken Rice Bake # 2	69
Classic Brisket of Beef	70
Corned Beef and Cabbage	72
Delicious Cheesy, Meat & Macaroni Casserole	73

Dilled Creamy Pasta	74
Easy Cheesy Spaghetti Chicken Bake	74
Easy Chicken Dish	75
Eggplant Au Gratin	75
Fettuccini Alfredo	76
Five Ingredient Brisket	76
Garden Pesto	77
Golden Corn Stuffing Bake	77
Ham & Eggs	78
Hamburger Corn Casserole	78
Impressionable Chick Flake Birds Nest	79
In Your Cupboard Chicken Casserole	80
Jelly Roll Chicken	81
Layered Ground Beef Casserole	82
Luncheon Meat Pie Special	83
Mexican Fiesta	84
More Please!	85
Mothers Southern Fried Chicken	86
One Skillet Beef Tenderloin	87
Oven Baked Salmon	89
Oven Crispy Chip Chicken Sticks	90
Oven Fried Chicken	90
Palm Crab Cakes	91
Pan Seared Salmon	92
Pork Chops	93
Pork Pastry Wellington	94
Salmon Croquettes	95
Salmon Delight	96
Salmon Noodle Casserole	97
Salmon Ovals	97
Salmon Party Log	98
Savory Molasses Chicken Breasts	99
Six Ingredient Chicken	100
Smoked Sausage Rice Skillet	101
Smothered Chicken	102
Steak with Caramelized Onions	103
Stuffed Eggplants	104

Sumptuous Meatballs — 105
Sweet & Savory Apricot Chicken with Potato Thins — 106
Taco Casserole — 107
Taco Pie — 107
Tuna Noodle Casserole — 108
Wasabi Salmon — 108

VEGETABLES & SIDE DISHES

Aunt Mallie's Baked Corn Casserole — 112
Better Than ChipsRoasted Potato Thins — 113
Carrot Casserole For Your Eyes — 114
Carrot Patties — 115
Sweet Potatoes Strudel — 116
Deborah's Southern Baked Beans — 118
Collards for Royalty — 119
Easy Halved Baked Potatoes — 120
Hawaiian Yams — 121
Holiday Favorite Green Bean Casserole — 122
Mac & Cheeses — 123
Mid-Eastern Baked Rice — 125
Sauteed Spinach — 126
Shoepeg Corn Casserole — 127
Skillet Potatoes with Herbs — 128
Southern Crumb Dressing — 129
Squash Casserole — 130
Steamed Cabbage — 131
Stuffed Squash — 132
Sweet Potato Casserole — 133
Traditional Cornbread Dressing — 134
Uncle Dan's Hopin Johns — 135
Vegetable Casserole — 136

BREADS & ROLLS

A Recipe For A Happy Day — 141
Banana Bread — 142
Banana Muffins — 143
Best Ever Spoon Bread — 144
Cheesy Onion Bread — 145
Cheesy Puff Pastry Twist — 146

Cinnamon Rolls	147
Coffee Cake	148
Doughnuts	149
Everyday Bran Muffins	149
Generational Quick Whipping Cream Biscuits	150
Hot Biscuits	151
Hot Rolls	152
Iris Nut Roll	152
Paper Thin Lacy Corn Cakes	153
Pop Overs	154
Pumpkin Pecan Bread	155
Scones	156
Scrumptious Scones	157
Spoon Bread	158

DESSERTS

A generational Favorite - Butter Nut Cake	164
5 Generation Wilson's Chess Pie Bars	166
A Desert for the Living	167
Apple Cake	168
Aunt Willa's Eclair Cake	169
Award Winning Brownie Cake	170
Award Winning Chocolate Buttermilk Frosting	171
Banana Pudding	172
Banana - Pecan Cake	173
Brownie Puddle Pie	174
Browned Butter Cake with Frosting	175
Buttermilk Pie	176
Chocolate Ganache Icing	176
Chocolate Leaves	177
Chocolatey Southern Pecan Pie	178
Coffee Ice Cream Pie	179
Cousin Amy's Cream Cheese Pound Cake	180
Easy Coconut Pie	181
Fanciful Fruit Pizza	182
Goof Poof Caramel Frosting	183
Goof Proof Frosting	184
Aunt Maudie's Lemon Meringue Pie	185

Grandma Stembridges Favorite Coconut Cake	186
Grandma Stembridges Pecan Pie	187
Great Grandma Lillie's Brownie Cakes	188
Great, Great Grandmas' Tea Cakes	189
Holiday Pumpkin Cake	190
Lime Pie Frozen Delight Treat	191
Mississippi Mud Cake	192
Mothers Old Time Southern Fruitcake	193
Mothers Peach Cobbler	194
My Prize-Winning Chocolate Sheet Cake	195
Cousin Linda's Oatmeal Meltaways	196
Over the Top Pecan Squares	197
Pecan Tastiest	198
Peach Pie Delight	199
Pineapple Cream Pie	200
Pineapple Delight Bundt Cake	201
Pineapple Treat	202
Royal Icing	203
Strawberry Cake	204
Strawberry Parfait	205
Sweet Nothings - Rugelach	206
The Best $150 Chocolate Coconut Cake	208
The Best Easy Fudge Frosting	209
Aunt Mallie's Toffee Squares	210

COOKIES & CANDY

A Recipe For Preserving Children	214
Aunt Maudie's Alabama Peanut Brittle	215
Buttery Pecan Turtles	216
Chocolate & Peanut Butter Truffles	217
Cookie Kiss	218
Crispy Ginger Snaps	219
Double Chocolate Treasures	221
Easy Lollipops	222
Florentine Cookies	223
Heavenly Chocolate Drops	224
Irresistible Chocolate Chip Cookies	225
Pecan Crunch	226

Cousin April's Reindeer Crunch	227
Snowballs	227
Sweet Pecan Sandies	228
Traditional Rocky Road Fudge	229
Ultimate Chocolate Brownies	230

THIS & THAT

A Must - Take Time For Ten Things	233
A Williamsburg Potpourri	234
Almond - Parmesan Cheese Spread	235
Basic White Sauce	235
Bubble Solution	236
Bubbles Galore	236
Canning Figs by Cousin Betty Clyde	237
Chicken Cream Sauce	238
Chicken Wraps	239
Child Play Dough (Not To Be Eaten)	240
Children's Hand Candles	240
Decorative Baskets & Ornaments	241
Finger Paints	241
Fricassee Sauce	242
House Seasoning	242
Kool-Aid Clay	243
Let It Snow	243
Mayonnaise	244
Mouth Watering Pecans	244
Open Faced Tuna Sandwhich	245
Recipe For A Happy Home	246
Seasoning In A Pinch	246
Silly Putty	247
Stain Remover	247
Vegetarian Open Faced Sandwich	248

INTRODUCTION

My cookbook was written by and for my mother and her mother in an effort to nail down recipes that were more oral tradition than anything else. Long before this book took written form, Robert married Ann and had three children Robert, Ann and Benjamin. He died a few days before Christmas in 1696 at his home on the Narrows of the Pequemons River. The oldest recipe is the one passed down called, Paper Thin Hoe Cakes. Originally, it was equal parts of corn meal and water, fried in bacon grease. Because of our health conscience culture, instead of bacon fat, we now use vegetable oil. Some of the recipes have been left in their original format and others have been tweaked to the preferences of friends and family.

As a child, helping out in the kitchen usually meant setting the table, clearing the table, sometimes licking the spoons from cake batters, tasting the blackberries for ripeness and getting a sliver of watermelon before taking it out to everyone on the back porch. It wasn't until one day, when Grandma was cooking chicken and dumplin's, that my Mother interrupted and said "wait Mother, let me get a spoon and measure out how much salt you're putting in that recipe." She told me to write down $3/4$ teaspoons of salt. I was making a grocery list for Grandpa to walk up to Grand Union, so paper and pencil was readily available. It was a logical but convoluted process in writing down the protocols for making chicken and dumplin's. And this is the day that it exactly all began.

Mother had instilled the values of love and laughter, along with the comfort of home cooked food, and the sincerest expression of love that builds the family. But home cooked food has to taste good and last till the next meal. Snacks were never encouraged. So every dinner and lunch included soup to nuts. Deserts were served individually. Even the adults seemed childlike as their piece was served and passed to them.

We were southern Americans which meant we enjoyed the slower pace so there was always time for family. Food was never the topic of conversation in these times, but one could not help but notice its inherent strengthening character. As time wears on and hectic schedules become chronic, one needs a resource book, like this cookbook, to hang on to and make it their very own and broaden the sunsets to something tolerable.

This forward was written to go along with the rest of the book. However grim, on June 2, 2007, early Saturday morning, there was a change. My mother and co-author of this book gently, and without warning fell asleep for the last time as we planned for things that never were to be. She has given all of us a sweet and invigorating heritage: providing sweet home making recipes. For everyone who knew my mother and for those who will love her recipes, we share them with you here. Sorry for the delay, you have all been so patient and so uplifting.

"Thank the Lord for these and

All thy many blessings, we humbly beg…"

Supper Prayer.

APPETIZERS & BEVERAGES

Tips for Appetizers and Beverages

⍟ Remember to keep your appetizers no longer than your pinky and not wider than a cracker. Miniature bite sizes are best.

⍟ If your party does not include dinner, plan on serving 6-8 appetizers per person. However, if you are serving a meal, prepare to serve 3-4 appetizers per person. Raw vegetables, fried Hors d' oeuvres, or frank and beans may be prepared ahead of time and refrigerated.

⍟ When serving appetizers or beverages, try to prepare ¾ of your planned food the day before or early in the morning so that you do not feel exhausted when guests arrive.

⍟ Pastry bags with cake tips that are filled with dips or creams can make decorative designs on toasts or crackers.

⍟ Keep your miniatures hot in the oven with a piece of aluminum foil spread loosely over the top in a 300 degree temperature.

⍟ Crudités is a French cooking term for fresh or raw vegetables that are cut or sliced into bite size pieces and served with a cold dip.

⍟ Out of sour cream or mayonnaise? Substitute yogurt or even spice up cottage cheese. Just remember not to beat the yogurt or c cottage cheese but stir the contents into the recipe.

⍟Quick Fruit Appetizers: Serve a platter or cutting board of grapes, sliced pears, sliced apples, apricots, figs, dates strawberries, fresh chunks of coconut, pineapple wedges or peaches, roasted peanuts, shelled pistachios, and caramelized pecans with wedges of good quality English blue cheese. Brie, Sharp American Cheese, or, and a variety of crispy crackers. Or slice the top of a fresh coconut, scoop out the coconut and drain the water. Fill the coconut shell with a mixed raspberry-poppy seed dressing, cream cheese and yogurt dip. Another great idea is to cut off the top of a pineapple, scoop out the insides of a pineapple, and prepare a dip of cream cheese, cottage cheese, pistachio instant pudding and a small can of crushed pineapple in its own juice. Sprinkle pistachio nuts on top. Garnish with mint, lemon leaves, fresh basil or Italian flat leaf parsley. (May be prepared within minutes of party or the day before.) Right before the party, we will sprinkle a little salt and drizzle extra virgin olive oil on the fruit. This really enhances the flavor of the fruit and gives it a fresh taste.

❈ Quick Vegetable appetizers: Serve a glass plate or platter of 3" sliced celery, carrots, green onion, broccoli, cauliflower, cherry tomatoes, cucumbers, mushrooms, radishes, green peppers, summer squash or zucchini. Cut out the center of a fresh raw green or red cabbage and serve prepared dip in the middle. Or group three different dips, one in red cabbage, one green cabbage and then cut out the center of a round pumpernickel onion loaf. Fill the center of each cabbage or bread loaf with different fillings such as almond cream dip, blue cheese dressing, mayo-ranch dressing, creamy salsa dip or a spicy Mexican dip.

❈ A quick festive non alcoholic beverage to serve with your appetizers is cranberry juice with sparkling non alcoholic carbonated white grape wine/juice. Or leave out the cranberry for a clean palate taste. Also you can serve sparkling cider which adds a little bubbly.

❈ Always try to chill or freeze your glasses or plastic drinking cups. It helps to keep the drink cold.

❈ Pour left over coffee into ice cube trays and freeze. This makes delicious coffee ice-cream shakes or iced coffee.

❈ Dissolve 2 vitamin C tablets in your orange juice to stretch the drink for a large crowd.

❈ Freeze lemon juice, or orange juice in ice cube trays. Add water, 1-2 teaspoons of sugar and 2-3 lemon or orange ice cubes. Stir well.

❈ If you are having expected or unexpected guest over and you just happened to fry your dinner or burn your dinner or have fish for dinner and you need to mask the smell in the house, quickly put on a full pot of French vanilla hazelnut coffee. The smell of the nuts with the vanilla and coffee give the home a homey smell.

❈ Saturate a clean cloth or cheese cloth with equal parts vinegar and water solution and wring almost dry. Wrap around the cheese. Then wrap in waxed paper and store in your refrigerator.

Miss Willadene's Fav's

A Party Time Mix

- 6 TBSP Land Lakes unsalted butter
- 1 tsp sugar
- 3 c. Wheat Chex cereal
- 1 TBSP Worcestershire sauce
- 2 c. Oh's Quaker Bran Cereal
- 1 tsp. seasoned salt
- 1 c. mixed nuts
- 2/3 tsp. garlic powder
- 1 c. toasted sesame sticks
- 2 c. Pretzel Sticks
- ½ tsp. onion powder
- 1 c. garlic- flavor bite size broken bagel
- 3 c. Corn Chex cereal chips, or pita chips

Pre heat oven to 250. Melt butter and sugar with nuts in a large roasting pan in oven. Stir in seasonings. Taste for adding more of a particular seasoning. Gradually stir in all ingredients until evenly coated. Bake for 1 hour, stirring every 15 minutes. Spread onto paper towels to cool. Keep for 2 weeks.

Beat the Clock Shake

- 6 oz. of orange juice
- 6 frozen strawberries
- 5 TBSP soy protein isolate
- ¼ of frozen banana
- 2 TBSP natural apple cider vinegar
- Non-caloric sweetener to taste
- 1 TBSP flaxseed oil
- 5 ice cubes
- 1 TBSP safflower oil
- ½ tsp. Optional: almond extract
- 2 TBSP soy lecithin flavoring
- 1 tsp. MSN powder
- ½ tsp. Optional: of vanilla extract
- 1 tsp. glutamine powder flavoring
- 1 4-6 oz container of vanilla yogurt
- 1/8 tsp of salt

In a food processor or blender, combine all of the ingredients until smooth.

Note: Encouragement is oxygen to the soul. - George M. Adams.

Best Ever Roasted Garlic Butter

10 roasted garlic cloves

½ cup olive oil

8 TBSP softened unsalted butter

1 loaf French Bread or Cuban Bread

In a baking pan, cut off the tops of 3 garlic bulbs. Drizzle with olive oil on cloves.

Bake in oven at 400 degrees for about 2 hours. Remove from oven, squeeze garlic cloves from their skin into a small bowl. Add the butter and stir until smooth. Spread on your favorite bread.

Note: My mother had a light brunch for the women's Bible study group. She served this dip as an appetizer. Even though these white gloved, prim and proper, bible thumping, southern women were afraid their breath would have the intoxicating smell of garlic, it didn't stop them from consuming every morsel of the spread.

Deborah Odom

Cheese Straws

1/3 c. lightly salted butter

1/4 tsp. salt

2/3 c. all-purpose flour

1/2 c. grated extra-sharp cheese

1/8 tsp. cayenne pepper

Preheat oven to 350. Put butter, flour, cayenne, and salt in bowl and work lightly with your fingertips until combined. Add cheese and mix thoroughly. Roll between floured wax paper to 1/8" thickness and cut into ½ " x 2" strips. Place 2" apart on baking sheet and bake until set and light brown about 12 to 15 minutes. Serve with one of the dips.

Note: These goodies are great on road trips. The natural ingredients are better for everyone instead of potato chips. You don't need to eat the whole package like you would with chips in order to be fully satisfied. You can eat one stick and feel satisfied.

Cheese Whip a la Roquefort

1 cup cottage cheese

½ cup Hellmann mayonnaise

¼ cup grated or crumbled Roquefort cheese

Place these ingredients in a bowl and whip with an electric mixer. Optional: crumble some crisp pork or turkey bacon on top.

Note: This is an excellent dip for potato chips, fried wings drum sticks or served as a dressing on a head of lettuce.

Deborah Odom

Chicken Hors D'oeuvre

- 1 ¼ pound boneless, skinless, chicken breasts (about 4 breasts)
- 2/3 cup firmly packed brown sugar
- 1 TBSP chili powder or curry or taco
- 1 pound package sliced maple flavored seasoning pork or turkey bacon
- 1 jar bleu cheese dip or dressing
- 1 cup of crushed pecan nuts or pine nuts.

Pre heat oven to 350 degrees. Cut each bacon sliced into thirds. Wrap each chicken cube with bacon and secure with a wooden pick. Mix together brown sugar and chili powder. Dredge wrapped chicken in mixture. Roll in crushed pine nuts or pecan. Spray a rack and broiler pan with nonstick cooking spray. Place chicken wrap on rack in broiler pan. Bake 350 for 30 to 35 minutes until bacon is crisp. Remove. Serve with vegetables and bleu cheese dip or dressing.

Chicken in Pastry

- 1 lb. of Boneless Chicken Breast
- 1 pkg. of 3 oz. of cream cheese
- ½ tsp. of salt
- 1 tbs of minced onion
- 1 to 2 TBSPs of milk
- 1/8 tsp of pepper
- 8 oz. pkg. of Croissant Rolls
- 2 tbs of melted butter
- ½ cup of seasoned crushed croutons

Heat oven to 350 degrees F. Cut chicken in to ¼ strips. Salt and pepper strips. Melt 1 tbs of butter and cook chicken in a skillet. Remove from heat. Add cheese, onion, milk and stir. Press 2 seams of crescent dough together and put ¼ of mixture in center and press all seams. Melt 1 tbs of butter and brush over triangles and sprinkle with croutons. Lightly grease a cookie sheet. Place triangle squares and cook for 20 minutes.

Deborah Odom

Cream Cheese Spread

4 oz. cream chesse softened

2 ¼ cups sifted confectioner's sugar

1 tsp. lemon juice

1 tsp. grated lemon rind

Combine all ingredients and mix well.

Exotic Cream Cheese Dip

1 cup Cream Cheese

Fruit or Vegetables

1 round onion

1 pkg. Good Seasons Salad Mix

½ cup sour cream

Mix and chill. Add food coloring for flare. Place dip inside a center carved out round pumpernickel onion bread. Use the center of the bread to make mini fruit & bread or fruit and vegetable shish kabobs. Get a decorative toothpick and layer a cubed pumpernickel bread, cucumber slice and repeat, ending with a grape; or layer cubed bread, pineapple wedge, repeat ending with a strawberry..

Note: Great with sticks of cucumber, pineapple wedges, whole strawberries and whole grapes.

FBI Frozen Thumbprints

- 1 stick Unsalted butter, cut into large
- ½ cup finely chopped black forest ham pieces OR SMOKED TURKEY
- 1 tsp. Molasses
- 1 cup shredded Cheddar, smoked Gouda or Gruyere cheese
- ½ tsp. Coarse salt
- 4 large eggs at room temp.
- 1 cup all purpose flour
- 36–½" cubes of Cheddar, Gouda or Gruyere cheese
- ½ tsp. freshly ground pepper
- 1 small jar of pimento

First, heat oven to 400 degrees. In a saucepan over medium heat, bring to a boil and stir in the butter, salt, molasses and 1 cup water. Vigorously, add flour until ingredients are combined. For about 1 to 2 minutes, over medium heat, continue to cook, and stir until the mixture pulls away from sides and a thin film forms on bottom of pan. Next, remove from heat and allow the ingredients to cool for about 2 minutes.

Transfer dough to a large bowl; add eggs one at a time, beating with a wooden spoon to incorporate each egg before adding the next, about 2 minutes. Stir in pepper, turkey or ham, and shredded cheese. Snip the corner of a sip plastic bag and insert a fitted ½ in star tip that you have lightly sprayed inside with Pam. Then, spoon dough into a plastic bag. On a flat baking sheet, use Silpat or parchment paper and pipe circular 1 ½ rosettes. Dampen your thumb and lightly press it in the middle to make a deep indentation. (During holidays, you may want to add food coloring.) Bake for about 25 - 30 minutes until crisp and golden. Press a cheese cube into indentation of each and remove thumbprints to a wire wrack. Serve immediately or freeze them by placing the cooked thumbprints on clean baking sheets; and freeze (uncovered) until firm for about 1 hour. Transfer to an airtight container; freeze until ready to use, up to 6 weeks. When ready to use, pre heat oven to 425 degrees and place thumbprints on an ungreased cookie sheet, baking for about 10 to 14 minutes. Serve warm. Garnish with chopped pimento.

Note: One of my mothers dearest friends is an assistant state attorney who loves my mother's cooking. She was having a housewarming party for some federal big wigs and wanted to have an elegant, untraditional finger food that would capture her guests. After all of these years, it is still the number one request at her parties.

Gingerale Fruit Punch

1 ½ qts. lemon juice (fresh)   1 qt. pineapple juice (fresh)

4 lbs. sugar   6 qts. water

1 ½ qts. orange juice (fresh)   2 qts. ginger ale

Mix first 5 ingredients together & let stand several hours on ice. Add 2 qts of ginger ale & pour over lime or lemon ice.

Note: This thirst quencher drink was loved by the young and old alike when it was prepared at our family reunions at the homeplace for the 4th of July.

Green Avocado Dip

3 Peeled and Pitted Avocados   1 TBSP minced onion

1 tsp. sugar   ½ tsp. salt

2 TBSP freshly squeezed lime juice   1 clove of minced garlic

¼ tsp. pepper

1 tsp. mayonnaise or yogurt

Mash avocados and lime juice with a fork. Stir in the rest of the ingredients. Salt and pepper to taste. Place mixture in the shells of the avocados. Serve on a bed of lettuce or shredded red cabbage. Top with cherry red tomatoes.

Note: Serve with toasted pumpernickle bread triangles, chips, crackers, or raw vegetables.

Deborah Odom

Party Cheese Ball

- 2 (8-oz.) pkg. softened cream cheese
- 1 tsp. paprika
- 1 pound Sharp Cheese
- 1 tsp. Worcestershire sauce
- 1 pound Mild Cheese
- 1 tsp. chopped chives
- 1 pound Velveeta Cheese
- 1 (16-oz.) pkg. chopped nuts
- 1/4 c. Finely chopped onions
- parsley

Use an electric mixer or food processor to blend all chesses together until smooth.

Add onion, Worcestershire, paprika, and chives. Mix well. Form into a ball and roll in chopped nuts and parsley. Wrap in plastic wrap, then foil to keep shape. Refrigerate until firm. To use, set out 30 minutes before the party.

Note: Variations: You might want to roll the shape into a log instead of a ball. Also, if you like a spicy cheese ball, add cayenne pepper to taste. Sometimes, I will replace 1 pound of Mild Cheese for ½ pound of Mild Cheese and ½ pound of Smoked Cheese. It is truly delicious...even on a saltine cracker.

Pastry Tomato Pizza

2 sheets frozen puff pastry, thawed

1/2 tsp. extra-virgin olive oil

2 egg yolks

1 tsp. sugar

2 tsp. corn oil

1/4 tsp. freshly ground black pepper

2 tsp. water

1/2 cup garden pesto (see recipe) or store-bought pesto

4 med. ripe tomatoes, sliced 1/4-inch thick

1 cup grated Gruyere cheese

Heat the oven to 400 degrees F. Prick the pastry with a fork so that it doesn't puff up during baking. Roll out the pastry on a lightly floured surface. Cut each sheet into an 8-inch circle, using a salad-size plate as a guide. Remove to an ungreased baking sheet. Prick the pastry all over with a fork. whisk together the egg yolks, corn oil and water; brush lightly on the pastry. Sprinkle 1 cup of cheese. Drizzle the pizza evenly with the olive oil, sugar and pepper. Bake about 25 minutes or until the tarts are golden and the tomatoes are caramelized. Serve immediately, with a dollop of Garden Pesto.

Note: This pizza bread dough reminds us of the pizza that we ordered when we went on a family vacation to Italy. Pizza in Italy is very different than pizza in America. The pizza dough in Italy seems to be more tasty than here in America. Definitely easier to chew. Although it makes a very little difference to Americans, I mean who doesn't like pizza?

Pineapple Lemonade

2 c. sugar

juice of lemons

2 c. water

2 cups fresh grated fresh ripe pineapple

Boil the sugar and water until it spins a thread. Cool. Add the lemon juice and grated pineapple. Add water to please-or ice, or crush in blender and sprinkle toasted coconut on top. Add food coloring.

Quick Baked Tortilla Chili Dip

1 (8-oz.) pkg. softened cream cheese

½ c. Sharp Cheddar Cheese

1 (15-oz.) can no bean Hormel Chili

1 bag Tortilla Scoop Chips or Pita Chips

½ c. Mozzarella Cheese

Pre heat oven to 350. In an 8 x 8 x 2 inch glass dish, spread cream cheese over bottom of pan. Next, layer with Hormel chili. Sprinkle with cheeses. If you want to repeat the layers, double the recipe. Bake about 20 minutes until hot and bubbly. Serve with your favorite chips.

Miss Willadene's Fav's

Uncle Bob's Pimento Cheese Spread

- 1 lb. of grated red rind cheese
- 8 oz. of grated Kraft sharp cheese
- 8 oz. of grated medium cheese
- 1 qt of Hellmann's Mayo
- Garlic and salt to taste
- Cayenne pepper to taste
- 3 medium jars of diced pimento (Pulverize in a food processor)
- 1 small jar of diced pimento

Use a hand mixer to combine first 4 ingredients. Add seasonings to taste. Serve. This recipe should be kept in a tight container for up to 2 weeks.

Vicky's Punch

½ bottle cranberry grape juice

¼ c. slivered almonds

2 whole cardamon

12 whole cloves

2 sticks cinnamon

1 box raisins

Put the first four ingredients in a cold pot. Bring to a boil. Boil over low for ½ hour.

Measure 2 tbs of raisins and almonds into a tea cup or mug. Then pour 1 cup of the hot mixture over the raisins and almonds in the tea cup. Place a saucer or lid over the cup and let it steep for 20 minutes before serving.

Whole Roasted Garlic

4 garlic bulbs, discard skins

8 sprigs basil, thyme, rosemary herbs

4 Tbs extra-virgin olive oil

Preheat oven to 425°. Slice in half a loaf of French Bread or Cuban bread and lather the tops of the cut slices in extra virgin olive oil and bake until toasted for about 10 - 20 minutes. Set the bread aside and prepare and bake the next ingredients. Cut a thin (¼ inch) slice from the top of each garlic bulb, if desired. Place bulbs and basil or herb of your choice in a baking dish. Drizzle each bulb with oil. Cover with foil; roast bulbs until soft and golden, at 425° for about 1 hour and 15 min. Spread the roasted garlic, (optional) soft cheese such as goat cheese, mozzarella, Velveeta on toasted bread.

Miss Willadene's Fav's

SOUPS & SALADS

Miss Willadene's Fav's

TIPS FOR SOUPS AND SALDS

❈ Plan on serving a half of cup of soup per serving.

❈ You can use a lettuce leaf to skim the fat off of soup or if you have time, refrigerate the soup and skim the fat off the cold soup. Just reheat the soup before serving.

❈ If your soup is too salty, add a whole boiled potato to the soup and then remove it.

❈ Bones are great for adding flavor to soups. Remember to remove bones before serving the soup.

❈ Soup broth or soup mixture can be frozen in freezer bags or ice cube trays.

❈ Chili is great frozen. I like to freeze the chili in ice cube trays and then remove them to a freezer bag. It makes it easier to serve the needed amount by thawing ice cubes instead of lumps of solid beef and beans

❈ The best croutons are make out of white bread that has melted butter generously drizzled over the top of it. Bake on a cookie sheet at 425 degrees. Check frequently. Remove when bread is crisp. THIS ALSO MAKES GREAT TOAST FOR BREAKFAST OR A LATE NIGHT SNACK. Very soothing to the stomach.

❈ ALWAYS wash salad leaves especially spinach leaves, even if packaging states its pre washed. We use baking soda or vinegar to a large basin of water and place the loose leaves in the mixture and stir slightly so that the dirt or insects fall to the bottom. Process may have to be repeated especially for endive, collards or any leafy vegetable. We actually clean all of our fresh vegetables and fruit in this manner.

❈ Perfect boiled eggs: Add 1 tablespoon of salt or white vinegar to cold water before adding the eggs. Let eggs hard boil for 5 minutes. Cover the pot and turn the heat off.

❈ Nuts can be kept fresh if you place the shelled nuts in a freezer bag and place them in your freezer. To heat up the nuts, we have put them in the microwave and it really does revive the taste of freshness within the nut.

❈ Freeze bananas in aluminum foil or baggies. Kids love the frozen bananas dipped in chocolate sauce and sprinkles or nuts.

❈ Freezing apples: Peel, slice or quarter apples and drop a few apples at a time into slightly salted cold water. Remove apples and immediately place them in a freezer bag or container.

❈ A molded salad can be easily removed if you spray the mold with cooking vegetable spray before filling the mold.

A Bouquet Garni

½ tsp. rosemary

2 crushed bay leaves

½ tsp. marjoram

1 tsp. thyme

½ tsp. parsley

4 inch square cheese cloth

Place rosemary, marjoram, parsley, bay leaves, and thyme in center of cheese cloth square. Bring corners of cloth together and tie with Rick-rack. Use in soups and stews.

Note: Not only will the bouquet flavor your food, but it will help your house smell good when your guest arrive. The aroma of the bouquet will give your guest the idea that you have been cooking all day. When I have prepared fish or fried food, I have even placed this bouquet in a pot of boiling water and let it simmer on the stove. It helped mask the offending odor.

Antipasto Salad

- 1 pkg. tri color cooked rotini
- 1 ½ c. parmesan grated
- 1 bunch fresh broccoli steamed
- ½ c. mayonnaise
- 1 can pitted black olives halved
- 1/2 c. Kraft ranch dressing
- 1 jar chopped of artichoke, drained
- ½ pkg. good seasons help dressing
- 1 level tsp. chopped red pepper dry package
- ½ whole chopped red onion

Mix - Toss all ingredients together-cover and put in refrigerator for at least 1 hour before serving.

Avocado Cream Salad Dressing

¾ c. mashed avocado

½ tsp. finely grated orange peel

1 c. heavy whipped cream

½ tps salt and pepper

½ c. confectioners sugar

Fold in avocado into whipped cream. Sift confectioners sugar and add to avocado mixture. Next add salt and pepper. Sprinkle the top with orange peel and if desired, finely chopped pecans or slivered almonds.

Deborah Odom

Black Cherry Congealed Salad

2 pkgs. Cherry jello

1 c. boiling water

1 can Pitted black cherries

1 tsp. sugar

1 cup Any kind of coke

1 can Crushed pineapple in heavy syrup

1 (8-oz.) pkg. cream cheese

1/2 can Pineapple juice

2/3 c. pecans

2 TBSP Mayonnaise

½ cup cherry juices

Dissolve jello in hot water. Cool slightly. Add cream cheese then coke and juices.

Congeal until mixture begins to thicken. Add fruits, sugar, pecans and mayonnaise.

Pour into mold. When salad is congealed firmly, turn out on dish of lettuce leaves.

Note: Kitchen Tip : A pinch of salt added to very sour fruits while cooking will greatly reduce the quantity of sugar needed to sweeten them.

Blue Cheese Salad Dressing

1 tsp. minced garlic

½ tsp. worstershire

¼ tsp. dry mustard

½ c. sour cream

½ tsp. black pepper

1 ½ c. mayo

1/8 tsp. white pepper

¼ c. buttermilk

2 Tbs red wine vinegar

1 c. good quality of crumbled blue cheese

Whisk red wine vinegar into all ingredients. The dressing will keep for four days in refrigerator.

Deborah Odom

Broccoli Salad

- 2 bunches broccoli
- ¼ c. sugar
- 1 c. raisins
- ½ tsp. salt
- 1 c. sunflower seeds or pecans
- ½ tsp. brown vinegar
- ¾ c. mayonnaise
- 1 large mixing bowl

Cut broccoli flowerets off into mixing bowl and add mayonnaise, sugar, salt, and vinegar. Mix well. Add raisins and sunflower seeds. Best to make in the morning for the evening meal. Stir a couple of times during the day.

Note: Whether you are cooking broccoli or using it in its natural state, in order to remove the strong odor of broccoli, soak broccoli covered in salty water for 30 minutes. Drain. Cook or leave in its raw form to dry before using in recipe.

Chicken Salad

4 cup diced chicken breast (cooked)

1 cup pecan pieces

1 (20-oz.) can of diced pineapple

1 cup mayonnaise (Hellmann's)

2 cup finely diced celery

1/4 tsp. All spice

1/2 tsp. Molasses

Mix all together and serve on bed of lettuce or in lettuce cup. Mandarin oranges can be substituted for the pineapple, and green grapes can be added to either.

Note: Easy and delicious. Great for the family picnics to the beach. Keep on ice.

Deborah Odom

Company Field Green Salad & Dressing

1 pkg. Washed & dried Field Greens Salad

1 cup Maple Syrup

1 cup crumbled Bleu Cheese

1 cup bottled Burgundy Poppy Seed Dressing

1/2 cup Toasted Pine nuts

1/2 cup Crumbled CRISP maple bacon

Place greens in salad bowl. Preferably a glass bowl. Whisk the Burgundy Poppy Seed dressing with the maple syrup. Pour liberally over the salad. Top with crumbled bleu cheese, bacon and pine nuts.

Note: One of our families favorite seafood restaurants is in Palm Beach, Florida. They have a terrific salad that we all love. Each time we went, we would all try to break down the recipe. We have finally mastered a recipe that I will guarantee you is now better than their recipe is. This recipe is pleasing to everyone. Be sure to fix plenty.

Your guests will beg for more.

Compliment Peach Salad

2 (3-oz.) pkg. of peach gelatin

1 cup of Dream Whip or heavy whipped cream

2 TBSP flour

3 ½ cup boiling water

1 egg slightly beaten

4 cups of canned peaches

1 (3-oz.) pkg. of cream cheese softened

1 cup syrup from can of peaches

1 cup chopped pecan nuts

½ cup of sugar

½ cup miniature marshmallows

Dissolve jello and chill until it begins to set. Fold in peaches and turn into 3 qt. casserole dish or mold. Chill until firm. In top of a double boiler, combine peach syrup, sugar, flour and egg. Cook over simmering water and stir constantly until thick. Cool. Fold in cream cheese and heavy whipped cream or 1 box of prepared Dream topping mix. (Follow directions for preparation on the box). Fold in nuts and the marshmallows. Spread on top of gelatin. Sprinkle with nuts and cheddar cheese. Chill 2 hours.

Note: This happens to be my favorite gelatin salad that my mother makes. On a hot summer day, we would cut a square of salad and eat it for lunch, a snack or even as a desert. It is refreshing.

Deborah Odom

Easy Summer Salad

- 1 No. 2 ½ can of pineapple chunks in heavy syrup
- 4 peeled shredded carrots
- 1 cup of chopped dates
- 1 cup of sliced celery
- 1 cup of chopped pecans
- 1 cup of sour cream

Drain pineapple; add remaining ingredients except sour cream. Chill and add sour cream just before serving.

Fight The Cold Chicken And Vegetable Soup

- 1 chopped large onion or leek (or 1 chopped bulb of garlic canned)
- 1 pkg. frozen mushroom barley soup
- 2 stalks chopped celery and celery leaves
- 1/4 tsp. all spice
- 2 stalks chopped carrots
- 3 TBSP butter
- 1 bunch of herbs: parsley, thyme and basil chopped
- 2 large chopped Idaho baking potatoes
- 1 chopped parsnip
- 1 chopped large turnip
- 1 tsp. salt
- 1 tsp. black pepper
- 1 qt. chicken stock

Place butter and onions, celery, garlic and carrots in pot. Heat and cook for 5 minutes. Then add the parsnip, turnip, potatoes, stock and soup. Bring to a boil. Cover and simmer for 1 and ½ hours. The last 15 minutes, add herbs, spices, salt, pepper and even sugar. Serve soup chunky or puree and pour a little dollop of fresh heavy whipping cream. Recipe may be frozen in freezer bags for up to 3 months.

Note: Drop a lettuce leaf into the soup and it will absorbed all of the grease/fat in the soup. Once it has served its purpose, remove leaf.

Deborah Odom

Four Ingredient Basic Salad Dressing

1 tsp. Kosher salt

Freshly ground black pepper

1 tsp. Dijon Mustard

1 cup Extra Virgin Oil

In a cone cup measuring bowl, add kosher salt and mustard. Twist black ground pepper 5 times. Stir. Let ingredients sit for two minutes. While vigorously stirring, drizzle extra virgin olive oil.

Ham Salad

- 1 can of diced ham or fresh chicken
- 2 hard boiled chopped eggs
- 3 TBSP of chopped sweet gherkin pickles
- 3 TBSP of chopped celery
- 1 small chopped apple
- 1 tsp of lemon juice
- ½ cup chopped raisins
- 1 cup of mayonnaise or salad dressing
- ½ cup of toasted sliced almonds
- Salt and pepper to taste

Combine all ingredients except mayonnaise or salad dressing; mix and add enough salad dressing to moisten. Chill. Serve on a red bib lettuce leafs and fresh hot buttered rolls.

Million Dollar Salad

2 eggs

No. 2 can drained pitted white cherries

5 TBSP melted butter

1 ¼ c. nuts

5 TBSP lemon juice

3 bananas (sliced)

½ lb. miniature marshmallows

½ pt. whipped heavy whipping cream

1 No. 2 can drained pineapple

Beat eggs, adding sugar, lemon juice, butter and marshmallows. Cook on top of double boiler until marshmallows are melted thoroughly. When cool, add to fruits. Fold in whipping cream. Chill in cold part of refrigerator for at least 12 hours.

Optional: Sprinkle lightly with shredded American cheese or toasted miniature marshmallows.

Note: My grandmother told me that she and her mother used to make this recipe with her grandmother. It seems to be over 200 years old. However, it is timeless. The ingredients are simple and readily available. Enjoy a piece of loving heritage that continues to span generations.

Mothers Five Star Corn Bread Salad

- 2 boxes Jiffy cornbread muffins mix(cooked,cooled,and crumbled)
- 2 whole tomatoes peeled, seeded, and diced
- 1 rib of celery diced
- 1 pt. mayonnaise(can use reduced fat mayonnaise)
- 8 slices crumbled cooked bacon or use turkey bacon
- 1 whole med. bell pepper chopped
- 1 c. green onion chopped

Mix all ingredients together and put in a large salad bowl. Cover with plastic wrap. This salad keeps for several days in refrigerator. It's even better after 2 days.

Note: If you do not try any other recipe in this book, try this one. I have never met a person who did not ENJOY this recipe. It will surprise you and impress your guests with the comforting taste of home. This recipe has my mother's trademark on it:. ...a bit of work - but made with tender loving care!

Ole' Taco Fiesta Soup

2 pound Ground Beef

1 TBSP Molasses

1 med. Onion, Chopped

1 cup water

1 can Chopped Green Chilies

½ tsp. Salt

1 can Undrained Kidney Beans

¼ tsp. Pepper

1 can Undrained Pinto Beans,

1 8 oz. box of melted Velveeta Cheese

3 cans Stewed Tomatoes

1 small carton of sour cream

1 pkg. Taco Seasoning Mix

1 bunch of green scallions

1 pkg. Ranch-style dressing mix (dry)

Brown meat and onion. Add all other ingredients and bring to a boil. Boil 3 to 4 minutes. Reduce heat and simmer 45 minutes. Add Velveeta. You can garnish individual servings with Tostitos, Fritos, chopped scallions, and a dollop of sour cream.

Note: Years ago, we took a family vacation to the Camelback Spas in Arizona. We ate a soup that was quite tasty but had too much hot and spicy and not enough of the true to form southern tradition of sweet and spicy. So, mother and I changed the recipe to give it a Southern flare.

Perfect Cole Slaw

¾ c. Hellmann's real mayonnaise

2 TBSP lemon juice

¼ c. whipped heavy whipping cream

1 tsp. salt

2 c. finely shredded cabbage green/ red mixed

1 c. finely shredded carrots

¼ c. finely chopped onions

2 TBSP sugar

¼ c. celery seeds

½ c. extra thinly sliced green and red peppers

Mix all the ingredients together. Optional: Add black pepper to taste. Cover and refrigerate for 1 hour or longer.

Note: I can picture the long buffet tables, white linens and mountains of food that was a part of my families desire to feed the masses of relatives. Who wouldn't want to eat a bowl of cole slaw, southern fried chicken, corn on the cob, baked beans, oh yea, and HOME MADE BISCUITS SLATHERED IN BUTTER AND HONEY??????????

Miss Willadene's Fav's

Pistachio Salad Delight

- 1 (3-oz.) box instant pistachio pudding
- 1 pkg. mini marshmallows
- ½ c. chopped pecans
- 1 (9-oz.) carton cool whip
- 1 No 2 can crushed pineapple and heavy syrup
- 1 (8-oz.) softened cream cheese
- 1/4 cup chopped green pistachio nuts

Mix all ingredients together and refrigerate for 30 minutes or more. Optional, add green food coloring. Top with chopped pistachio nuts and sprinkle with mini marshmallows.

Note: College student, beginning chef or salad critic! Anyone can quickly make this salad, in which these simple ingredients make it easy to prepare.

Ranch Dressing in a Pinch

- 1 Minced Clove of Garlic Mashed
- 1/4 cup Mayo
- 1 tsp. Dry Mustard
- 1/2 cup Buttermilk

Mix all of the ingredients together. Store in a tightly concealed container. Refrigerate for up to 2 weeks.

Shrimp Salad

- 2 pound medium shrimp cut in large chunks, cooked.
- 2 cups small sweet green peas
- 2 tsp. garlic (fresh and minced)
- 2 cups celery diced
- 1 pound angel hair or thin spaghetti, cooked as directed
- 1 qt. mayonnaise
- 1 large jar diced pimentos
- 1/4 tsp. of each: salt, pepper & sugar

Combine cooked pasta and garlic and set aside. Add shrimp, celery, and peas. Then add mayonnaise and fold in pimentos. Add salt, pepper and sugar.. Allow to cool in refrigerator up to 3 hours before serving on bed of lettuce.

Note: You can substitute smoked fish or salmon for the shrimp.

Sweet Macaroni Salad

1 TBSP butter

1 c. finely chopped green & red peppers

1 tsp. prepared dijon mustard

2 TBSP sugar

¼ tsp. pepper

1 tsp. salt

1 c. thinly sliced celery

1 (8-oz.) pkg. elbow macaroni (cooked

¼ c. chopped onions drained)

2 tsp. sweet pickle juice

¾ to 1 c. Hellmann's mayonnaise to taste

In a bowl mix all the ingredients together. Refrigerate for 30 min to 1 hour.

Thousand Island Salad Dressing

1 c. mayo

1 chopped hard boiled egg

1/4 c. chili powder

1/4 c. pimento stuffed olives

1 tsp. minced bell green pepper

1 tsp. white sugar

1/4 c. minced onion

Mix all ingredients together, keep for 4 days in refrigerator.

Note: My grandmother and mother always had their favorite home made dressings around. This just happens to be my grandmothers favorite.

Tuna Salad In Its Edible Bowl

1 cup of white meat tuna in can of water

½ cup of water

1/4 cup of butter

½ cup of all purpose flour

Salt

1 tsp caraway seeds

3/4 cup of Mayonnaise

1 TBSP of pine nuts

2 eggs

1 cup of chopped lettuce hearts

1 tsp lemon juice

1 TBSP of minced onion

Paprika to taste or

Optional: curry powder to taste

8 carrot curls

Preheat oven to 400 degrees F. Bring water and butter to a boil in a heavy saucepan. Add flour, dash of salt and caraway seeds. Stir vigorously over low heat for about 1 minute or until mixture leaves side of pan and form a ball. Remove from heat; cool for about 10 minutes. Add eggs one at a time beating until smooth after each addition. Spread batter evenly in a greased 9-inch glass pie plate. Do not spread batter up side of plate. Bake for about 45-50 minutes. Cool slowly away from drafts. Puff will form a bowl high on side and flat in the center. Combine tuna, celery, lettuce, and lemon juice, and onion, dash of salt, paprika or curry and moisten with mayonnaise. Fill puff just before serving and top with pine nuts and carrot curls. Use a peeler and slice the length of the carrot into thin slices. Curl and refrigerate to set.

Miss Willadene's Fav's

Whipped Cream Dressing

2 cups stiffly whipped cream

1 cup mayonnaise

Fold mayonnaise into whipped cream.

Salt to taste.

Note: This dressing is great tossed on lettuce, fresh or canned fruit, or even on a slice of warm toasted onion pumpernickel bread.

Deborah Odom

MAIN DISHES

Deborah Odom

TIPS FOR MAIN DISHES

* FREEZING TIPS FOR MEAT: Chicken can be frozen up to e months; beef, veal and lamb up to 10 months and pork or ham up to 5 months.

* FREEZING TIPS FOR SEAFOOD: Lobster and crabs up to 2 months; fatty fish, oysters, scallops, and clams up to 3 months; shrimp and lean fish up to 6 months.

* Thaw meats in the refrigerator to retain its juices. Meats can go directly from freezer to heat but it will take twice as long to cook.

* When boiling seafood, add celery leaves to the water to reduce the odor.

* All meat is easier to carve if you remove it from the oven and allow it to rest for 15 minutes.

* Chicken is cooked when you are able to wiggle the drumstick with ease from the body of thechicken.

* Before roasting meat, grease the pan with oil so that the juices do not burn.

* Easy perfect roast chicken: Wash, salt and pepper a chicken, add all spice, dry poultry seasoning powder, basil and garlic powder generously all over chicken. Place a pierced orange or lemon in the cavity of the chicken and place the uncovered chicken breast side down in pan and sprinkle potatoes, carrots, celery, onion and whole garlic with butter and place these vegetables around the chicken. Cook breast side down at 450 degrees for 45 minutes. Turn chicken right side up and cook an additional hour at 350 degrees. DELICIOUS!!!

* Check your fresh fish to be sure that the eyes are clear, the gills are pink, and the scales are shiny and the fish is void less of smell.

* Never put hot food in a cold slow cooker. Heat the slow cooker first before adding hot ingredients.

* Vinegar is a great meat tenderizer. Just add vinegar to water in which you are boiling the meat. Only add about 1 teaspoon of vinegar to water.

❈ Place a waxed paper liner between the saucepan and the lid to keep foods from burning or drying out. Keeps the liquid in the pan.

❈ When we make stuffed peppers, we put the green peppers in a greased muffin tin.

❈ Inexpensive meat can also be tenderized if you cook it in tea instead of water.

❈ To deepen brown gravy, stir in a small amount of instant coffee.

Deborah Odom

How To Preserve a Husband

1 Loving wife   1 Available Husband

Be careful in your selection- They are better if not fresh. Some choose them young, others want them old; - but that is a matter of personal taste. Do not boil; many insist on keeping them in hot water, but this always makes them sour and hard. Be careful not to chill with indifference - instead keep them warm with the sunshine of smiles.

Even the poor varieties may be made sweet, tender and good if spiced with the essence of love and fair play. If treated this way they will keep forever.

1-2-3- Chicken and Rice Bake

- 1 cup of cooked rice
- 1 can of onion soup
- 1 cut up fryer chicken
- Salt and Pepper to taste
- ¼ tsp of curry powder
- 1 TBSP of chopped flat leaf parsley
- 1 can of cream of celery or chicken soup
- ½ cup of shredded Cheddar Cheese

Pre heat oven to 325 degrees. Sprinkle rice into a greased baking casserole dish. Mix soups, water, salt and pepper and cheese with chicken. Spread over rice. Sprinkle parsley. Bake uncovered for 1 hour and 30 minutes.

Deborah Odom

Baked Chicken Breast

6 - 8 Chicken Breast

1 can water

1 c. cream of chicken soup

1/2 stick butter

1 c. uncooked white rice

1 pkg. Lipton dry onion soup

(16-oz.) can mushrooms

Brown chicken lightly in butter. Sprinkle rice on the bottom of buttered casserole. Add chicken soup diluted with water, sprinkle onion soup over mixture. Arrange chicken and mushrooms on top. Cover and bake at 300 degrees for 1 hour and 15 minutes.

Baked Pasta with Sausage

- 1 (16-oz.) pkg. smoked sausage (beef, pork, turkey, or chicken)
- 1 grated bulb of garlic
- 1 celery stick finely chopped
- 1 1/2 c. milk
- 1 green pepper finely chopped
- 4 c. cooked penne pasta
- 1 c. frozen peas in a box
- (8-oz.) pkg. pasta
- 1 c. thinly sliced carrot sticks
- 1 c. shredded mozzarella cheese
- 1 1/2 c. cheddar French fried onions in a can
- 1 c. parmesan cheese
- 1 finely chopped onion

Heat oven to 350 degrees. Saute in 2 tbs of butter or olive oil, onions, peppers, garlic, and celery. Add sausage. Drain. Combine soup and milk in a 3 qt. Casserole dish. Stir in pasta and sausage mixture, ½ a cup of cheese, ½ a cup of French fried onion rings, peas and carrots. Bake for 30 minutes until hot. Stir. Top with cheese and onions.

Deborah Odom

Baked Red Snapper

- 1 lb. skinless red snapper fillets
- 1 TBSP lemon juice
- 1/2 tsp. soy sauce
- 1 TBSP orange juice
- 2 TBSP gated onion
- 1/8 tsp. pepper
- 1 TBSP grated orange rind

Place fillets in a shallow baking pan that has been sprayed with non stick coating. Combine onion, lemon, orange juice, and pour the fish. Cover and refrigerate 30 minutes. Sprinkle fish with soy sauce and pepper. Bake in a moderate oven at 450 degrees for 8 to 10 minutes. Garnish with slice of green pepper and sprinkling slices of almond, twist of lemon or pineapple. Slice with cherry in the middle or shreds or raw carrot and a mint leaf. Add 1 seasoning of cinnamon and cloves or parsley and ginger.

Note: Throughout the year, a family tradition was to go on a fishing trip with multitudes of relatives. Not only did we spend all day catching loads of fish, we spent the evening, cleaning, cooking and eating these mouthwatering treats of specks, brim, flounder or bass.

Baked Salmon Cheese

- 1lb can of drained flaked red salmon
- 3 eggs separated
- 2¼ cup of milk
- 1cup of soft bread crumbs
- 1 cup of shredded Cheddar Cheese
- 1 tsp of minced onion
- 1/2 tsp of soy sauce
- 1 tsp of salt
- 1/8 tsp of pepper
- 1tsp of lemon juice
- 3 TBSP of butter
- 3 TBSP of flour
- 2tbsp of chopped dill

Preheat oven to 350 degrees f. Beat egg yolks with ¾ cup of whole milk. Add bread crumbs, cheese and onions, ½ tsp of soy sauce, pepper and 1 tsp of lemon juice with salmon in a large bowl. Mix well. Beat egg whites until stiff, fold into salmon mixture. Turn mixture into a shallow 1 qt baking dish. And bake for about 30 minutes. Melt butter in saucepan and blend in flour and salt. Remove from heat; stir in remaining milk gradually. Cook over medium heat, stirring constantly, until thickened. Cook for 1-2 minutes longer. Stir in dill. Serve over salmon.

Beef in a Skillet

- 1 egg lightly beaten
- ¾ cup of fine soft bread crumbs
- ½ cup of catsup
- 2 TBSP of minced onion
- 1 tsp of salt
- 1 tsp of Worcestershire sauce
- 1 lb of ground beef chuck
- 2 TBSP of olive oil
- ½ cup of chopped onion and 1½ cups of thinly sliced onion
- 1 cup of thinly sliced celery
- 3 cups of sliced thin potatoes
- 1 ½ cup of sliced carrots
- ½ cup of diced green pepper
- ½ cup of diced red bell pepper

Sauté, ½ cup of onions, and peppers until tender. Cool. Combine egg with crumbs, catsup, cooked minced onion, peppers and 1 teaspoon of salt, and Worcestershire sauce. Add beef and mix thoroughly with a fork. Shape into thick 6 inch patties. Place patty in center of skillet with oil and brown. Sprinkle remaining sliced onion around beef. Brown beef on both sides, turning carefully with pancake turner and spatula. Stir onions frequently as beef browns. Arrange separate groups of potatoes, carrots, and celery in large second skillet. Add ½ cup of water; sprinkle with remaining salt. Cover; parboil for 5 minutes. Serve hot.

Barbecued Chicken in a Bag

1 frying chicken cut up.

Salt and pepper to taste

6 TBSP of catsup

2 TBSP of vinegar

1 TBSP of lemon juice

2 TBSP of Worcestershire sauce

4 TBSP of water

1 stick of butter

4 TBSP of brown sugar

1 tsp of soy sauce

2 tsp of dry mustard

1 tsp of chili powder

½ tsp of red pepper

Preheat oven to 500 degrees. Season chicken with salt and pepper. Combine remaining ingredients in a saucepan and bring to a boiling point. Grease inside of large paper bag; place bag in roaster. Dip each piece of chicken in hot sauce and place in a bag. Fold bag down from top. Fasten with paper clips. Place lid on roaster and bake at 500 degrees for 15 minutes. Reduce heat to 350 degrees and bake for 1 hour and 15 minutes longer.

Deborah Odom

Beef Stroganoff

2 lb. sirloin steak

1 pt. sour cream

(8-oz.) mushrooms

3 TBSP flour

1/4 c. butter

1 can condensed beef broth

3/4 c. onion

1 garlic clove minced

Cut steak ¼ inch thick. Cut into strips ¼ inch wide. Brown meat quickly in small amount of fat, and remove meat from skillet. Add mushroom and onion & garlic.

Cook until tender, but not brown. Add beef broth. Heat to boiling. Blend sour cream with flour. Stir into broth. Return meat to skillet, and stir until thickened. Add salt and pepper to taste. Serve over hot rice.

Best Chicken & Dumplings

Chicken : 1 {2 1/2 } pound chicken ,cut into 8 pieces

1/4 c. garlic mined

1 qt. chicken broth

1 cup of minced onions

2 cups of celery, chopped

Dumplings:

1 c. of ice water

2 c. all purpose flour

2 bay leaves

1 TBSP. salt

ice water

2 chicken bouillons

1 {10 3/4 - ounce } c. condensed cream of mushroom or chicken soup

Put the chicken, celery, onion, bay leaves, bouillon, All spice and garlic in a large pot. Next add 3 quarts of water and chicken broth and bring to a simmer over medium heat. Cook chicken on low heat for 40 minutes. Remove the chicken from the pot. Cool and debone the chicken. For Dumplings: mix the flour with the salt and mound together in a mixing bowl. At the center of the mound, drizzle a small amount of ice water over the flour. By hand gradually mix in ¾ cup of ice water. Knead the dough into a ball. Sprinkle a cup of flour onto a clean work surface. With a rolling pin, roll out the dough about 1/8 inch thick. While dough rests, add the cream of chicken to the pot from the chicken and simmer gently over medium low heat. Use a ruler and measure to cut the dough into 1 inch pieces. Cut dumpling in half and add to soup mixture. Slowly move the soup mixture and dumplings in a circular motion so the dumplings cook evenly. Cook until the dumplings float and are no longer doughy, 3 to 4 minutes. Return the chicken pieces to the pot and gently stir to incorporate.

Note: Every true southern lady knows how to make five things: fried chicken, dumplings, cornbread, grits and sweet tea.

Broiled Flounder

1 lb. flounder

3/4 c. milk

1 TBSP Dijon style mustard

1/4 fresh dill

1 TBSP butter

1/8 tsp. black pepper

2 TBSP fresh lemon juice

1/3 c. plain low-fat yogurt

1 TBSP all purpose flour

1 minced garlic clove

1/2 tsp. soy sauce

Place flounder in baking dish. Sprinkle with lemon juice, spread with half mustard. Refrigerate for one hour. Pre heat boiler. Coat the boiler rack with nonstick spray. Broil flounder on rack 5 to 6 inches from heat at 8-10 minutes. In the meantime, prepare a sauce to go over the flounder. Melt butter, whisking flour, soy sauce. Cook for 2 minutes. Whisk in milk, and cook until thickened for about 4 minutes. Stir in dill, remaining mustard and pepper. Whisk mixture into the yogurt. Serve over dish.

Chicken & Dumplings # 2

6 chicken breast

1/2 cup milk

Dumplings 1 chicken bouillon cube

2 cup self rising flour large pot

1/3 cup shortening

In water and bouillon boil, skin, and debone chicken. Keep stock. Add salt and pepper to taste. Dumplings: In bowl pour flour, shortening, add milk to make dough stiff.

Roll out on floured board about 1/8" thickness. Cut into 1 inch squares and sprinkle generously with flour. Drop into boiling stock slowly. Cover and boil on medium heat for 8 to 10 minutes. Return chicken to stock. Stir

Note: For quick and handy seasoning while cooking, keep on hand a large shaker containing six parts of salt and one of pepper and a smidgen of garlic powder.

Chicken and Rice Bake

1 can chicken soup

1 1/2 cup water

1 can cream of mushroon or cream of celery soup

3/4 cup rice cooked

dash paprika

1 can fried onion rings

dash pepper

4 chicken breast

Heat the oven to 375 degrees F. In a 3 qt oblong baking dish, combine chicken, soup, water, rice, and pepper or paprika. Bake at 375 degrees for 1 hour until chicken is done. Top with remaining onions. Bake for 3 minutes or until its golden brown.

Chicken Croissant

4 breast of chicken

1 cup grated cheddar cheese

2 cans of Pillsbury crescent rolls

1 can cream of chicken soup

1 cup whole milk

Heat oven to 350 degrees F. Pull chicken off bones; Place chicken on the wide end of the croissants and roll up to the small end. Bend ends and place in casserole dish. Mix milk, cheese, and soup. Pour over the croissants. Bake for 40 to 45 minutes uncovered.

Good Neighbor Casserole

2 lbs. Boneless chicken breasts (cooked and sliced)

1/2 Lemon Juice

2 tsp. Curry Powder

1 1/2 lbs. broccoli (trim and separate into spears, steam until partly cooked)

1 tsp. Butter

1 cup Cheddar Cheese, (grated)

1 cup cooked carrot midgets

1/2 cup Dry Bread Crumbs.

1 can Campbell's cream of chicken soup

1/8 tsp. black pepper

1/3 cup Mayonnaise

Heat a 350 degree oven. In a large baking casserole dish, cut broccoli spears to the same size and lay across the dish, with the flower heads facing the sides of the dish.

Next, lay the shredded pieces of the chicken and cooked carrot midgets on top of the spears. Mix the condensed soup, mayonnaise, lemon juice, and curry powder. Spread across the chicken layers. Sprinkle cheddar cheese on top of mixture. Melt the butter in a bowl, add bread crumbs, and mix to coat the. It should still be crumbly. Sprinkle bread crumbs on top of the cheese this may be kept in the refrigerator until ready to bake. Bake for about 20 to 30 minutes.

Note: One of our neighbors had just moved in next door and they had 7 children. They were tired from moving; little ones were crying, parents were anxious and dinner was a guess. My supermother took them this hearty, delicious, warm casserole. She even remembered the paper goods, ice and of course garbage bags. They never forgot it.

Deborah Odom

Chicken in a Bottle

8 to 10 chicken breasts

1 pack Lipton onion dry soup mix

1 cup Russian dressing

dash salt

1/3 cup small jar apricot preserves

Heat oven to 300 degrees F. Place chicken breasts in shallow baking dish, and use a little regular salt besides. Combine next 4 ingredients and pour oven chicken. (I usually double the sauce recipe.) Bake covered in a 13 x 9 x 2 inch pan for 2 hours.

Serve with rice. Garnish with slices of pineapple, apricot halves, and parsley.

Miss Willadene's Fav's

Chicken Mushroom Pie

1 can of drained mixed vegetables

6 tiny pearl white whole onions

1 can of cream of mushroom soup

½ cup of whole milk

3 cups of diced cooked chicken

2 tbsp of chopped parsley

1 pkg. of refrigerator biscuits.

Preheat oven to 450 degrees. Cook vegetables in small amounts of boiling salted water until tender; drain. Combine soup and milk in saucepan; heat to boiling. Add vegetables chicken and parsley; pour into 1 ½ qtr casserole. Top with biscuits. Bake for 15 minutes or until biscuits are browned.

Chicken Parmesan

1 egg

1/4 cup Olive Oil

1 1/2 tsp. milk

1/3 cup Chicken Broth

1/8 tsp. salt

2 TBSP White Cooking Wine

1 clove garlic, crushed

2 TBSP Fresh Lemon Juice

4 skinless boneless chicken breast

11/4 cup Grated Fresh Parmesan or Mozzerella Cheese

1/2 cup of Italian seasoned bread crumbs.

Heat oven to 350 degrees F. In a shallow dish, stir together egg, milk, salt, pepper and garlic. Pound chicken breasts with mallet to flatten then, dip in egg mixture and roll in the bread crumbs. In a large skillet, heat olive oil over medium heat, the cook the chicken in skillet until golden brown, turning once. Drain on paper towels. Then arrange chicken in large baking dish. In a small mixing bowl, combine chicken broth, wine, and lemon juice. Pour over chicken. Sprinkle with Parmesan cheese, cover and bake for 25 minutes. Uncover and bake for 10 minutes. Garnish with lemon wedges and parsley and serve.

Chicken Pie

1 fryer boiled	1 c. self rising flour
1 3/4 cups chicken broth	3/4 c. flour
1 can cream of chicken soup	1 c. milk
3 boiled eggs sliced	1 stick of butter

Grease baking dish. Place soup and chicken stock in dish. Layer chicken and sliced eggs. Mix flour and milk in melted butter. Pour over chicken mixture and bake at 350 degrees until bubbly and brown.

Chicken Rice Bake # 2

2 chicken breasts	1 TBSP red pepper (chopped)
2 c. rice	2 c. water
1/2 tsp. salt	1 tsp. salt
1 TBSP onion (chopped)	For Rice: skillet
1/4 tsp. black pepper	

Cook the chicken breast in the 2 cups of water, until done. Set aside and cool. When they are cold, chop them in pieces. Fry the onion and the red pepper in oil. Stir in the rice, chicken and the consomme. Cover and cook on low heat until done.

Classic Brisket of Beef

- 1 7 to 10 pound whole USDA choice brisket, point and flat intact, with ½ inch fat covering
- 1 bottle Heinz Chili Sauce
- 1 env. Lipton's onion soup mix
- 1 (16-oz.) cans coca-cola
- 2 tsp. fresh minced garlic

The first day, preheat oven or electric roaster for 20 min. at 350 degrees. Brisket can be taken right from the refrigerator it does not have to be at room temp. Pour the chili sauce, onion mix and the cola into a bowl and mix. Don't be tempted to taste this, its awful! Dump the mixture over the brisket, lifting the brisket to let some of the liquid spread under it. Cover and roast until the flat portion of the brisket is fork tender, from 2 to 3 hours. The meat should be tender, but still give a slight tug as you pull a fork out of the brisket. If it is not fork tender, cover brisket and return it to the oven, checking at 15 minutes intervals. When the brisket is done, remove it from the roaster, and allow cooling at room temp. On a platter. When the gravy has cooled, pour it into a container and refrigerate. Wrap the cooled brisket in plastic wrap and place in the refrigerator overnight. Once refrigerated, the roasted brisket and cold gravy can remain there 3 to 5 days before slicing, reheating and serving. The next day, trim off all visible fat from the cold brisket, turn it over and place on a cutting board. The lean side of the brisket should be what you are looking at. Look for the grain the muscle line of the brisket indicated by lines on the meat.

With a sharp knife, slice the brisket across or against the grain. If the slice appears stringy, you're slicing the wrong way. Remove the gravy from the refrigerator. Remove the fat and discard. Heat the gravy in a saucepan until it boils. Pour over your brisket slices, cover the roaster and reheat your brisket for 1 hour at 350 degrees.

Deborah Odom

Corned Beef and Cabbage

½ cup of chopped flat leaf Italian parsley

1 cup of finely sliced celery

1 large chopped green pepper

1 large onion chipped

1 tsp of fresh minced garlic

2 tsp of canola oil

1 can of corned beef crumbled

1 2 lb, of cabbage

1 large can of tomatoes

1/4 cup of Worcestershire sauce

1/8 tsp of light soy sauce

¼ tsp. of pepper

Sauté parsley, celery, green peppers, onion and garlic in oil in a large deep pot for about 5 minutes. Reduce heat to low and add corned beef. Cut cabbage in to eighths; separate cabbage leaves. Place in pot. Add tomatoes, Worcestershire sauce, soy sauce and pepper. Add enough water to cover cabbage. Bring to a boil and then reduce heat to medium. Cover. Cook for about 30 minutes

Delicious Cheesy, Meat & Macaroni Casserole

1 pound Box elbow macaroni

1 tsp. all spice,

2 TBSP vegetable oil

2 TBSP Molasses

2 cups chopped green bell pepper

1 tsp. dried basil

2 cups chopped onions

1 Tbs of lite soy sauce

1 TBSP chopped garlic

1 8 oz grated mozzarella

2 pounds lean ground beef. or turkey or chicken

8 slices of provolone cheese

1 8 oz. grated cheddar cheese

3 cups canned crushed tomatoes or fresh

Heat the oven to 350 degrees F. Cook the macaroni according to package directions; drain and set aside. Heat the oil in a skillet; add the peppers, onions, and garlic, and saute until soft. Add the ground beef and saute until browned. Drain the beef on a paper towel to remove excess grease. Add the tomatoes, salt and pepper, all spice, soy sauce, and molasses in a large bowl, and combine the macaroni and the beef mixture. Add 1½ cups of cheddar + 1 cup of mozzarella. Top with the provolone and bake for 20 to 25 minutes, or until the cheese is lightly browned and bubbly.

Note: Everyone should bake this dish at least once. This is one of my childhood favorites. If you follow the recipe, it will be tasty time, after time, after time.

Dilled Creamy Pasta

2 TBSP heavy cream

salt and pepper

1 TBSP butter

1 TBSP chopped fresh dill

2 cups fully-cooked egg noodles

In a saucepan heat cream and butter over low heat, add noodles, and seasoning with salt and pepper. Toss until well mixed and heated through. Remove from heat and toss in dill. Serve immediately.

Easy Cheesy Spaghetti Chicken Bake

4 Chicken breasts

1 can of chopped seasoned tomatoes (Italian) (Vinegar etc.)

1 can of Cream Mushroom soup

1 pound of sliced Velveeta Cheese

1/4 cup of finely grated onion

1 pkg. of Angel Hair or regular Spaghetti

Pre heat oven to 350°. Next, boil chicken breasts until tender. Debone chicken and cut into bite size pieces. Boil spaghetti in leftover chicken broth and drain. Mix all ingredients except for 6 slices of cheese in a deep 13 x 9 x 2 casserole dish. Place remaining cheese on top of casserole. Cover with aluminum foil and bake for 30 minutes.

Easy Chicken Dish

1 c. chopped cooked chicken

1 c. grated cheese

1 c. chopped celery

1/3 c. mayonnaise

1 can cream of chicken soup

1 c. cooked Veg.

1/2 c. grated cheese

Combine all ingredients. Top with cheese and crushed corn flakes bake at 350 degrees for 30 min.

Eggplant Au Gratin

1 med eggplant

½ cup of chopped onion

¼ cup of chopped green pepper

1 can of chopped tomatoes

1 egg slightly beaten

Pepper to taste

1 cup of grated sharp cheese

¼ cup of parmesan cheese

1 cup of cracker crumbs

¼ cup of butter

Preheat oven to 350 degrees F. Peel and slice egg plant. Salt slices and drain them on a paper towel for 30 minutes.

Cook until tender in salted boiling water. Drain. With a fork, smash into small pieces. Add onion, green pepper, tomatoes, egg and pepper. Arrange alternate layers of eggplant mixture, cheeses and cracker crumbs in a 1 qt greased casserole dish. Bake for 30 to 40 minutes.

Fettuccini Alfredo

1 pound fresh fettuccini noodles

3/4 cup fresh grated Parmesan cheese

6 Tbs butter

1 stalk of finely chopped chives

1 cup heavy cream (room temperature) saucepan

Cook fettuccini in salted boiling water until tender, about 10 minutes. Drain water, add grated cheese, butter and cream. Mix thoroughly, serve.

Five Ingredient Brisket

4-6 lb. beef brisket

1 bottle wishbone Italian salad dressing

3 bay leaves

1 cup water

1 bottle Worcestershire sauce

In large pan, put bay leaves under brisket. Add 1 cup water, 1 bottle Worcestershire sauce, 1 bottle Wishbone dressing and marinate overnight. Bake at 250° for 6 hours.

Garden Pesto

2 cups fresh basil leaves

2 TBSP grated parmesan salt and pepper, to taste

4 TBSP minced garlic

2 TBSP pine nuts

1/2 tsp. molasses

1/3 cup extra-virgin olive oil

Chop the basil, garlic and pine nuts in a food processor. With the motor running, drizzle in the oil. Blend in the cheese, molasses, salt and pepper. Refrigerate, covered, for up to 3 days. Makes about 1 cup

Golden Corn Stuffing Bake

1 can of golden corn soup

4 Chicken Breast sliced 1/4 inch

1 1/2 cans of cornbread stuffing

1 tbs of molasses

1/4 cup of chopped onion

1 tbs of melted butter

1/4 cup of finely sliced celery

1 tsp of brown mustard

1/2 tsp. soy sauce

Heat oven to 400 degrees F. Combine soup, stuffing, celery, onion, soy sauce and spoon on to a greased 9 inch pie plate. Press chicken into cornbread mixture. Next combine soy butter, mustard and molasses. Spoon over chicken. Bake for 25 minutes

Ham & Eggs

1 cup of diced cooked ham

2 hard boiled eggs sliced

2 cups of thick white sauce

Buttered bread crumbs

1 cup of grated Cheddar Cheese

Salt and Pepper to taste

Preheat oven to 400 degrees f. Layer ham and eggs and cheese in casserole. Add half the white sauce and repeat the layers. Top with bread and remaining cheese. Bake until golden brown.

Hamburger Corn Casserole

1 lb. ground beef

1 can cream mushroom soup

1 large onion chopped

1 (2-oz.) jar diced pimento (drained)

1 (16-oz.) can creamed corn (drained)

2 1/2 c. grated cheddar cheeses (divided)

In a skillet cook beef and onion until tender (drain), combine with corn, soup, pimento, and 2 cups of cheese. Pour into a greased 2 qt casserole and sprinkle ½ cup of cheese over the top. Bake 350 degrees for 30 to 40 minutes. Serve with rice.

Impressionable Chick Flake Birds Nest

4 medium sized Idaho potatoes

solid Crisco oil

5 cups chicken cream sauce

4 cups cooked white chicken cut into cubes

Peel and grate or shred potatoes with a vegetables shredder with 3/8" round holes. Line a strainer (4' diameter at top) with the shredded potatoes using only enough to thinly cover the inside of the strainer. Place another strainer (2 diameter at top) inside of the first strainer which will help the potatoes stay in place. Set the strainer down in the hot deep fat and fry until golden brown. Remove and tap or help the nest out of the bottom strainer urging with the blade of a knife. Allow to cool and reheat in oven just before serving the chicken flakes in the shell. Combine the chicken flakes and cream sauce add additional seasonings if desired and reserve in the nest and creams.

Deborah Odom

In Your Cupboard Chicken Casserole

- 1 6 oz can of deboned white meat chicken
- 1 can of cream of chicken soup
- 1 cup of diced celery
- 3 tsp of minced onion
- ½ cup of chopped pecans
- ½ tsp of soy sauce
- ¼ tsp of pepper
- 1 TBSP of lemon juice
- ¾ cup of mayonnaise
- 3 hard-boiled eggs, thinly sliced
- 3 cups of crushed potato chips
- 1 cup of grated Cheddar Cheese

Preheat oven to 450 degrees. Drain and dice chicken. Reserve broth. Combine chicken, broth, soup, celery, onion, pecans, soy sauce pepper, lemon juice mayonnaise, cheese and eggs. Spoon into a 1 qt baking dish and sprinkle with potato chips and cheese. Bake for 15 to 20 minutes or until golden brown.

Jelly Roll Chicken

1 ¼ cup of self rising flour

½ cup of Crisco solid shortening

1 egg beaten

3 TBSP of milk

1 cup of diced cooked chicken

½ cup of minced celery

2 TBSP of minced flat leaf parsley

1 ½ tsp of soy sauce

1 can of cream of chicken soup

½ cup of Cheddar Cheese

Preheat oven to 375 degrees F. In a food processor, combine flour, shortening, egg and milk, pulsing until mixture dough forms into a ball. Chill dough. Combine chicken, celery, parsley, soy sauce, and half the soup. Mix well. Divide dough in 2 parts; roll each part to a rectangle. Spread with chicken mixture; roll dough as for jelly roll, sealing ends. Place in greased baking pans. Bake for 25 minutes. Combine remaining soup and ½ cup of water, and cheese in sauce pan. Stir over low heat until well blended and serve over chicken.

Deborah Odom

Layered Ground Beef Casserole

1 1/2 c. peeled, cubed potatoes
1 lb. lean grown beef
1 c. chopped bell pepper
1 c. chopped onion
1 1/2 c. peeled, sliced carrots
1 1/2 c. tomato juice

Grease 2 quart. Casserole layer potatoes, carrots, onions and bell pepper. Spread raw beef over vegetables pour tomato juice over all. Bake 350° for 1 hour.

Luncheon Meat Pie Special

1 ½ pkg. of frozen mixed vegetables

½ cup of chopped onions

¼ cup of diced green pepper

2 TBSP of butter

1 12 oz can of luncheon meat

1 cup of evaporated milk

2 tsp of flour

1 cup of grated Cheddar Cheese

2 eggs beaten

½ tsp of soy sauce

¼ tsp of paprika

1 unbaked pie shell

Preheat oven to 400 degrees F. Cooked frozen vegetables. Drain. Combine onion, pepper and butter in sauce pan and simmer covered for 10 minutes. Meanwhile, cut luncheon meat into ¼ inch slices and reserve 5 slices. Cut remaining slices into bite size pieces. Add small amount of milk to flour mixing into smooth paste; combine four mixture, remaining milk, vegetables, and onion mixture and bite size luncheon meat, cheese, eggs, soy sauce and paprika. Mix well. Pour into pie shell. Halve reserved luncheon meat slices diagonally and arrange over top of pie. Bake for 35 to 45 minutes. Cool for 10 to 15 minutes before serving.

Mexican Fiesta

- 1 can of Cream Corn
- 1/4 cup of finely chopped green pepper
- 1 can of Rinsed Blackbeans
- 1 pkg. of flour tortillas
- 1 can of Stewed tomatoes
- 1 pkg. of crushed corn chips
- 1 can of Cream of Chicken Soup
- 1 tsp. of thick molasses
- 2 oz. Cream Cheese
- 2 cups of Mexican Blend shredded
- 1/3 cup Sour Cream cheeses
- 3 cooked and deboned chicken breasts
- 1 tsp. salt
- 1/2 cup of finely chopped onions

Pre heat oven to 350°. Saute onions and pepper in a little butter until translucent. Except for tortillas and cheese, add all of the remanding ingredients over low heat until bubbly. In a rectangle pan lightly oiled with olive oil, layer tortillas, creamed chicken mixture, then cheese and continue layering until you end with cheese on top. Bake for about 30 minutes or until bubbly. What makes this recipe tasty and flavorful is when you buy all named brand products. For example, Del Monte Creamed Corn, Bush's Blackbeans, Hunts or Del Monte's Tomatoes, Philadelphia Cream Cheese, Breakstone Sour Cream, Fritos Corn Chips and Grandmas Molasses. Why is it so important? Because I have found that other not as well known brands do not have the pungency of taste which is what this dish is all about.

More Please!

- 1 pound lean hamburger
- 1 tsp. molasses
- 1 onion chopped
- 1 can mushroom soup
- 1 can tomato soup
- 1 (8-oz.) pkg. Wide noodles cooked and drained
- 1 can peas (drained)
- 1 large box Velveeta cheese
- 1 can whole kernel yellow corn drained

Heat oven to 350 degrees f. In a skillet, brown hamburger. Remove beef from skillet and drain on a paper towel or brown bag. Next, drain access fat in skillet and add onions. Brown the onions and return the beef to the skillet. Add remaining ingredients. In a 13 x 9 x 2 inch rectangular pan, layer noodles and sauce twice. Grate Velveeta cheese over the top of the casserole. Bake for 25 minutes or until cheese is melted.

Note: This is a crowd pleaser. Mother could take this dish for Wednesday night suppers on the grounds and there would not be a drop left. Some liked this dish better than its counterpart, Lasagna. At the end of the supper, one almost thought that someone had washed the pot.

Deborah Odom

Mothers Southern Fried Chicken

2 quarts Crisco solid vegetable shortening

2 TBSP white cornmeal

2 TBSP salt

3 2 1/2 pound frying chicken

2 tsp. ground pepper

2 cups flour

a pinch of paprika

Heat shortening in a well seasoned cast-iron skillet to 375°. The temperature is very important. Wash and lightly salt and pepper chicken the night before. Cut each into 8 serving pieces. In a large mixing bowl, combine four with cornmeal, salt pepper and paprika; Dredge chicken and set on a paper towel. Fry chicken in hot oil turning to brown evenly on all sides.

This will take about 10 to 12 minutes. Remember that your white meat will cook faster than dark meat so you may want to cook your white meat last. As each piece becomes golden brown and tender, set on a brown paper bag to drain. Keep chicken hot until serving in a pre heated oven at 350°.

Note: Even a queen will be tempted to forgo the fork and knife.

One Skillet Beef Tenderloin

- 1 1/2 pounds beef tenderloin, trimmed and tied
- 1 cup canned beef stock
- 1 TBSP Dijon mustard
- 2 tsp. coarse salt
- 2 tsp. grainy mustard
- 1 tsp. freshly ground pepper
- 1 TBSP brown sugar or molasses
- 1 TBSP olive oil
- 2 TBSP unsalted butter
- 8 oz. shallots (3 large), peeled and cut into 1/4-inch-rounds
- 1 cup all purpose flour
- 1/2 A small handful of Italian flat parsley
- 2 TBSP balsamic vinegar

Heat oven to 425°. Mix salt, pepper and flour together. Roll all of the beef in the flour mixture. Place a skillet with an ovenproof handle over medium-high heat, and add olive oil. When very hot, add meat; and brown. Place the skillet of beef into oven for 10 minutes. Add shallots to pan; return to oven for 15 to 20 minutes more. Remove beef from skillet and let it rest on a cutting board for at least 10 minutes. While beef is resting, make the fabulous spicy mustard sauce. In the same skillet, over medium-high heat, deglaze the skillet of shallots by adding balsamic vinegar. Be sure to use a wooden spoon to stir all the browned bits from the bottom of the skillet. Next, add the stock, and simmer until slightly reduced, 2 to 3 minutes. Reduce heat to low, and stir in sugar, mustards and butter. After the beef has rested for al least 10 minutes,

Deborah Odom

cut beef into ½-inch-thick slices and top with the sauce and shavings of parsley.

Note: Everyone looked forward to the Sunday meal after church. This recipe could be prepared the day before or the morning of. The intoxicating smell of beef tenderloin that resides in your home for hours to come, will leave your family with a smile. (Leftovers if any are great as Philly Cheese Steak Sandwiches.)

Oven Baked Salmon

- 1 lb. of skinless salmon
- 1 skinless, seedless medium tomato
- 1 tsp. olive oil
- 1 onion
- 1 TBSP lemon juice
- 1 tsp. parsley
- 1 clove garlic
- 1 tsp. oregano
- 1 tsp. salt
- 1 TBSP canola oil
- 1/4 cup bread crumbs
- 2 TBSP butter
- 1/4 cup pine nuts optional

Combine oil, lemon juice, garlic, and salt. Cut salmon in 4 equal parts. Rub oil mixture on salmon. Cover and refrigerate for 30 minutes. Take salmon uncovered and sprinkle bread crumbs and the butter on top of salmon. Bake 12-15 minutes until flaky. Garnish with tomato mixture. Dice skinless, seedless tomato and chopped onion. Add diced tomato onion, parsley, oregano, that was sauteed in canola oil for 2-5 minutes. Spoon tomato mixture on tip of cooked salmon. Top with ½ tsp of mayo, sour cream, or yogurt.

Oven Crispy Chip Chicken Sticks

2 lbs. chicken breast cut into long strips

3 cloves garlic

1/8 tsp. black peppers

1/4 tsp. of parsley

1/4 tsp. salt

1 1/2 c. frosted flakes or potato chips

1 c. extra light virgin olive oil

The meal serves 6-8 people. The time to cook is 20 minutes and the ovens temperature is 375 degrees. Place cereal in another bowl. Mix garlic, pepper, parsley, salt, and olive oil in blender for 2 minutes. Dip chicken strips in garlic and then in cereal. Place in a single shallow pan. Drizzle remaining garlic mixture over chicken and sprinkle remaining chips or cereal.

Oven Fried Chicken

2 c. Cans of corn flakes

1 fryer

salt or pepper

1 c. pet milk

Wash and cut up fryer. Salt or pepper. Crush corn flakes. Dip chicken in pet milk and roll in corn flakes. Place chicken in a pan lined with aluminum foil. Then cover with foil bake at 300 degrees for 45 minutes.

Note: CLEAN OVEN: to remove burned food from oven, place small cloth saturated with ammonia in oven over night, and food can be easily wiped up.

Palm Crab Cakes

(makes 3 dozen)

- 1 Tbs unsalted butter
- 1/2 tsp. freshly ground black pepper
- 10 Tbs olive oil
- 1/2 pound lump crabmeat, drained and picked to remove shells
- 1 small red onion, finely diced
- 1 small red bell pepper, finely diced
- 1 small green bell pepper, finely diced
- 1/4 cup finely chopped fresh basil
- 4 stalks celery, finely diced
- 1/2 cup mayonnaise
- 1/2 tsp. Worcestershire sauce
- 2 tsp. Dijon mustard
- 1/2 tsp. soy sauce
- 2 L eggs, lightly beaten
- 3/4 cup bread crumbs

In a large skillet, heat butter and 2 tablespoons olive oil over medium heat. Add onion, bell pepper, celery, Worcestershire sauce, soy sauce and pepper; saute until the vegetables have softened, 8 to 10 minutes. Let cool to room temperature. Transfer the cooled vegetable mixture to a medium bowl. Add crabmeat, breadcrumbs, basil, mayonnaise, mustard, and eggs, and stir to combine well. With your hands, shape mixture into 2-inch patties, about the size of a woman's palm. In a large saute pan, heat 4 tablespoons olive oil over medium heat. Add 8 to 10 crab cakes, and cook until golden brown, 1 to 2 minutes, on each side. Drain on paper towels. Towels. Plate and serve.

Pan Seared Salmon

- 2 5 oz. fillets salmon, cut on the bias into thin long fillets
- 2 tsps of McCormicks All Season Spice
- 1 tsp of molasses
- 4 TBSP olive oil
- dilled creamy Pasta, for serving (see next recipe)
- 3/4 cup breadcrumbs
- 1/4 cup Parmesan cheese
- 2 TBSP fresh chopped herbs (such as parsley, dill and chives)

Wash salmon- Rub 1 tsp of all season spice and 1 tbsp of olive oil into salmon. In a shallow bowl combine breadcrumbs, Parmesan, herbs, salt and pepper, and 1 tablespoon of olive oil. Dredge fillets in breadcrumb mixture, pressing firmly to make crumbs adhere. In a medium saute pan heat remaining 2 tablespoons olive oil over medium-high heat and carefully add salmon. When first side has formed a golden crust, turn carefully, reduce heat to low and cook 3 minutes more. Serve salmon on bed of dilled pasta.

Pork Chops

2 tsp. melted butter

4 tsp. prepared mustard

1 tsp. salt

1/2 c. water

6 pork chops of 1 1/2 thick

2 tsp. worestishire

1/2 c. ketchup

1/8 tsp. cayenne pepper

Heat oven to 350 degrees F. Mix butter, salt, ketchup, mustard, water, worestishire and pepper together. Pour sauce over chops and add water and cover. Bake for 2 hours.

Deborah Odom

Pork Pastry Wellington

1 tsp. chopped fresh rosemary

1 TBSP olive oil

1/2 tsp. salt

1 sm. chopped onion

1/4 tsp. black pepper

2 cloves garlic

1 lb. pork tenderloin

(16-oz.) bag baby spinach

1 thawed pastry puff frozen sheet

1/4 tsp. salt

Egg Wash

1/4 tsp. black pepper

1 egg

3 TBSP Dijon Mustard

1 TBSP water

2 tsp. sugar

Heat oven to 450 degrees. Heat oil in filling in a medium size skillet over medium heat. Add onion and garlic. Cook 10 min. Until softened. Add spinach, salt pepper then cook until spinach is wilted and liquid evaporates, 3 to 5 min. Remove from heat, add mustard. Next, mix rosemary, salt and pepper in small bowl. Rub over pork. Open pastry sheet on lightly floured work surface. Roll out to at least 12 inch. length. Spoon onion spinach mixture, into 3 inch wide mound down center. Place pork on top of spinach mixture, Folding over tail end. Wrap pastry over tenderloin to cover - tuck in ends under pork. Make 3 slashes in top of pastry. Brush pastry with egg wash. Transfer to ungreased rimmed baking sheet. Bake for 35-45 min.

Salmon Croquettes

1lb can of drained red salmon

½ cup of soft bread crumbs

¼ tsp of grated onion

Pepper to taste

¼ tsp of Worcestershire sauce

1 tsp of soy sauce

½ can of cream of mushroom soup

Cornmeal

Crisco solid oil

Combine bread crumbs, onion, pepper, soy sauce, Worcestershire sauce, and soup and stir in salmon. Mix well. Shape salmon mixture into croquettes and roll in cornmeal. Chill for 2 hours. Fry in hot solid Crisco oil until browned.

Salmon Delight

1 can pink salmon

1/2 c. chopped green pepper

1/2 c. mayonnaise

1 can cream of celery soup

1 beaten egg

1 tsp. lemon juice

1 c. dry bread crumbs

1 tsp. salt

1/2 c. chopped onion

Heat oven to 350 degrees F. Mix all ingredients together. pour into a baking pan and bake for one hour.

Note: The odor from baking or boiling salmon may be eliminated by squeezing lemon juice on both sides of each salmon steak or on the cut surface of the salmon and letting it stand in the refrigerator for one hour or longer before cooking.

Salmon Noodle Casserole

1 1/2 cup of white sauce

2 cans of flaked salmon drained and deboned

1 cup of cooked noodles

a dash of soy sauce

1/4 cup of Ritz cracker crumbs

a sprinkle of black pepper

Heat oven to 375 degrees F. Drain and flake salmon. Fill a well oiled baking dish with alternate layers of salmon, white sauce and noodles. Be sure to season each layer.

Cover the top with Ritz Crackers. Bake in oven for 30 minutes.

Salmon Ovals

2 c. flaked salmon

1 tsp. butter

3/4 c. course crackers

1 tsp. ketchup

1 egg slightly bitten

1/2 tsp. woresteshire

1 small onions sliced

1/2 salt

Mix salmon, cracker crumbs, and beaten egg together. Saute onion in butter and add to salmon mixture. Add seasonings. Shape into thin oval cakes and brown in 2 tbsps of butter.

Salmon Party Log

1 lb. red salmon

1/4 tsp. salt

1 (8-oz.) pkg. cream cheese

1/4 tsp. liquid smoke

1 TBSP lemon juice

1/2 chopped fine pecans

2 tsp. grated onion

1/8 tsp. garlic powder

3 TBSP snipped parsley

Drain and flake salmon, remove skin and bones, Combine next 6 ingredients and mix well. Combine parsley and pecans. Shape salmon into "8 x 2 " log. Roll in nuts. Chill and serve on crackers.

Savory Molasses Chicken Breasts

1/2 c. fresh orange juice

freshly ground black pepper to taste

3 TBSP ketchup

6 skinless boneless breast halves (about 6 ounces)

1 tsp. brown sugar

2 TBSP each molasses and honey

2 TBSP each peeled and minced fresh ginger and garlic

1/2 tsp. All spice

Make marinade, bowl, combine all ingredients except chicken. Add chicken and toss with marinade. Let rest, covered, at room temperature for 30 minutes, of refrigerate, covered for 2 to 3 hours. Preheat the oven to 350 degrees. Fahrenheit. Remove the chicken breasts to a shallow baking pan to fit and pour the marinade over the breast.

Bake for 30 minutes or until cooked though, basting often with the pan juices.

Remove the chicken to a plate. Pour the pan juices into saucepan and bring to a boil, reduce until thickened. Serve with the chicken.

Deborah Odom

Six Ingredient Chicken

4 (6-oz.) boneless, skinless chicken breast halves, tenderloins removed

1/3 c. grated parmesan

6 TBSP unsalted butter or margarine

1 1/2 c. fine fresh bread crumbs

1 minced clove of garlic

Flatten chicken breasts between sheets of plastic wrap to 3/8 inch. thickness in 9 inch pie plate or large shallow dish, combine bread crumbs and grated cheese. In cup, on high power, microwave 2 tbsp butter until melted, about 20 seconds, stir in ¾ tsp salt and ½ tsp pepper. working with 1 breast at a time, place butter side down, in crumbs, press down to coat. Brush top of breast with butter, turn over and coat with crumbs.

Place on waxed-paper-lined baking sheet. Repeat with remaining breasts. In each of 2 large non stick skillets, melt 1 tbsp butter until foamy. Place 2 chicken breasts in each pan, cook over medium heat for 6 minutes, turning once, until coating is golden brown and chicken is cooked though (adjust heat if crumb mixture is browning too quickly). Remove chicken to serving platter, wipe one of the skillets clean. In clean skillet, melt remaining butter, cook over medium heat until light golden and smells toasted. Stir in lemon juice and garlic pour over chicken. Serve with sauteed escarole, if desired.

Miss Willadene's Fav's

Smoked Sausage Rice Skillet

1/2 sliced carrots

1/4 tsp. thyme leaves

1 cab (8-oz.) stewed tomatoes drained

(16-oz.) smoked sausages cut into pieces

1 med. onion length wise sliced

1 1/2 c. cooked instant rice

1 TBSP butter

1/2 onion

1 c. water

1/2 green pepper

1/4 tsp. basil leaves

Saute carrots, onions, pepper in a 10 inch skillet with butter over medium heat for 3 minutes. Add tomatoes with juice, water, basil, thyme, and sausages. Bring to boil.

Reduce heat to low, cover and simmer for 5 minutes. Stir in rice, cover, remove from heat and let stand for 8 minutes, stirring after 4 minutes.

Deborah Odom

Smothered Chicken

2 1/2 pound broilers or 4 chicken breasts

shortening - Crisco solid

1 c. flour

2 c. fricassee sauce

salt and pepper

Heat oven to 350 degrees. Wash and dry broilers and dust lightly with flour salt and pepper. Fry in hot shortening in a heavy skillet until light brown, Remove and drain.

Place in a pan. Pour fricassee sauce over and cover and bake at for 1 hour or until done.

Miss Willadene's Fav's

Steak with Caramelized Onions

- 2 boneless sirloin steaks(each about 1pound and 1/2 inch thick)
- 1 garlic clove,minced and mashed into a paste
- 1/2 tsp. sugar
- 5 1/2 TBSP extra virgin olive oil
- 1 3/4 pound small red onions,halved lengthwise and cut into 1/3-inch-thick wedges
- 3 TBSP balsamic vinegar
- coarse salt and freshly ground pepper

Place steaks on a large plate, and rub with garlic paste and 2 tablespoons oil,coating completely. Season generously with salt and pepper. Set aside to marinate 15 minutes at room temperature. Meanwhile, in a large skillet, heat 2 tablespoons oil over medium- high heat until hot and just starting to smoke. Reduce heat to medium; add onions, and cook, stirring occasionally, unit softened and golden brown, about 7 minutes. Add sugar, vinegar, and 2 tablespoons water; simmer stirring occasionally, until opinions are tender, about three minutes more. Transfer onions to a bowl, and season with salt and pepper. Set aside. Wipe skillet clean. Heat remaining 1 ½ tablespoons oil in skillet over height heat until hot but smoking. Cook steaks until golden brown, about 2 minutes per side for medium-rare. Transfer to a cutting board, and let rest 5 minutes before slicing.

Note: Carving is unduly complicated by a dull knife, and remember the first rule of carving "cut across the grain" if you cut with the grain, long meat fibers give a stringy texture to the slice. Steaks are exception.

Stuffed Eggplants

2 med. eggplants flour for dredging

1 Tbs of finely chopped parsley

2 eggs, beaten

2 cups marinara sauce

grated cheese (if desired)

1/2 pound sliced mozzarella

1 pound ricotta cheese

2 Tbs olive oil

Preheat oven to 350. Wash eggplants, remove stems, peel and slice lengthwise. Dredge eggplant in flour. Dip into beaten egg and fry until golden brown. Pat dry with paper towels. Place a slice of mozzarella in the middle of each eggplant slice. Add a scoop of ricotta. Roll up eggplant slices's and place eggplant rolls, seam side down, in greased shallow baking pan and top with a little Marinara sauce. Bake for 15 to 30 minutes. If desired, garnish with chopped parsley, and grated cheese. Great with pasta on the side.

Sumptuous Meatballs

2 1/2 popunds round steak

1 tsp. garlic powder

1/2 cups finely chopped onions

1/4 tsp. pepper

1 whole egg

1/2 cup of heavy cream

1 TBSP cornstarch

2 TBSP flour

1 tsp. salt

3 cups of thin cream

Have butcher to grind meat. Mix egg, onion, cornstarch and seasonings. Mix in cream. Lightly mix in the meat. Shape into small balls about the size of a plum. Brown these carefully in a skillet of butter or chicken fat over low to medium heat. Remove from skillet, stirring the drippings, and 2 tablespoons of flour. Stir rapidly to avoid burning or lumping. Add 3 cups of thin cream. Pour this over meatballs and bake in covered dish for 1 ½ hours in a preheated oven of 350°f. Serve with noodles or mashed potatoes. *The use of an electric mixer to whip up the mixture before shaping into meat balls will give you a lighter product..

Sweet & Savory Apricot Chicken with Potato Thins

- 4 Skinned and boned chicken breast halves
- 2 tsp. vegetable oil
- 6 green onions, thinly sliced Roasted Potato Thins
- 1/4 tsp. Salt
- 1 (16-oz.) can Apricot halves, undrained
- 1 large unpeeled baking potato vegetable cooking spray
- 1/2 cup Orange juice
- 1 TBSP dark sesame oil
- 2 TBSP lite soy sauce
- 1/4 tsp. molasses
- 3/4 cup all-purpose flour
- 2 minced garlic cloves

Heat oven to 400 degrees F. Place chicken between 2 sheets of plastic wrap. Flatten to ½ inch thickness, using a meat mallet or rolling pin. Sprinkle with salt. DRAIN Apricots, reserving liquid. Coarsely chop apricots. STIR-together reserved liquid, apricots, juice, and soy sauce, garlic, molasses, and sesame oil. Combine flour and pepper; dredge chicken in flour mixture. COOK- Chicken in hot vegetable oil in a large skillet over medium-high heat to medium; stir in apricot mixture. Cook 3 to 5 minutes. Add onions and cook 1 minute. Sprinkle with fresh Italian parsley. CUT-potato into thin slices; arrange on an aluminum foil-lined baking pan coated with cooking spray. Lightly coat slices with cooking spray. Sprinkle with salt and pepper. Bake for 30 minutes or until golden brown.

Taco Casserole

1 lb. ground beef.

1 (16-oz.) c. stewed tomatoes.

2 (5-oz.) pkg. yellow rice (Spanish Flavor)

1 c. cheddar cheese soup.

1 can diced tomato with chili

1 pkg. taco mix

1 c. grated cheddar cheese.

Cook meat and drain, add taco mix to melt, cover rice and add cheese soup and tomatoes to rice mix well, and place in baking dish in layers. starting with rice, add a layer of meat, a layer of rice, etc, until you have used it all. Sprinkle with grated cheddar cheese. Bake until hot or until cheese has melted.

Taco Pie

1 can chili

grated cheddar cheese

1 small onion, diced

1 bag dip size Fritos

casserole dish

Heat oven to 350 degrees F. Butter a 13 X 9 X 3 inch casserole dish. Layer in the following order: Fritos, chili, onion, and cheese. Repeat this order until all ingredients are used up. Make cheese the last on top. Bake until the cheese is bubbly.

Tuna Noodle Casserole

- 1 (6-oz.) pkg. noodles
- 1 (7-oz.) can tuna
- 2 cups white sauce
- 3 TBSP chopped Italian parsley
- 2 large eggs
- 1/2 cup buttered bread crumbs

Cook noodles in boiling salted water until tender. Make white sauce. (I use the Gold Medal WONDER to make the white sauce.) Beat eggs slightly; add to sauce. Add tuna to egg sauce. Arrange alternate layers of sauce and noodles in buttered baking dish. Sprinkle each layer with parsley. Top with bread crumbs. Bake for 30 minutes at 350 degrees.

Wasabi Salmon

- 1 filet and skinned salmon at least a foot long
- 1 tsp. of dill
- salt & pepper to taste
- 1 whole lemon

Heat oven at 400 degrees F. Line a baking pan with aluminum foil. Place washed and dried salmon in pan. Brush salmon with melted butter and add salt and pepper to taste.

Squeeze 1 lemon. Sprinkle with dill. Bake in oven for 12 minutes.

Miss Willadene's Fav's

VEGETABLES & SIDE DISHES

TIPS FOR VEGETABLES

❊ Always salt and pepper the water before adding your vegetables. Use chicken or beef broth to boil your vegetables. Try to boil/cook your vegetables in as little water as possible.

❊ FREEZING VEGETABLES: Except for lettuce, cabbage tomatoes, and potatoes, most other vegetables can be blanched and frozen for up to 8 months in the freezer.

❊ Mother always kept a freezer bag of sliced onions, yellow, red and green peppers in the freezer.

❊ A perfect baked potato is washed, pierced, rubbed in butter or oil and then in kosher salt.

❊ Before peeling, slicing or chopping an onion, place the onion in the freezer for 15 minutes.

❊ To easily remove the skin of tomatoes or peppers, dip them in boiling water for 30 seconds.

❊ Want fluffy rice? Use 1 teaspoon of lemon juice for each quart of cooking water.

❊ Gradually add pasta to rapidly boiling water. Drain pasta in a colander but do not rinse.

❊ Clean your vegetables with equal parts water/vinegar solution, baking soda and a vegetable brush.

❊ Parsley, basil, mint and lemon leaves can be kept fresh in freezer. Place leaves in ice cube tray, fill with water and freeze. Remove frozen cubes and place in a freezer bag. Remove cubes from freezer and use in heated cooking dishes or thaw in a heated glass dish with a smidgen of warm water.

❊ Burned Beans? Remove beans from scorched pot, and place them in a clean saucepan with a little bit of liquid. Place a slice of bread of toast on top of the burned beans and continue cooking.

❊ While cooking spinach, use a chicken or beef bouillon to add flavor.

❊ Water in your vegetables boiling over? Add a teaspoon of butter to the water.

Deborah Odom

Aunt Mallie's Baked Corn Casserole

- 2 17 oz. cans of creamed style corn
- 1 medium bell pepper chopped
- 2 medium onions finely chopped
- 1 tsp of molasses
- 1/2 tsp of crushed pepper
- 1 c. of Ritz crackers
- 2 eggs
- 1 c. of American or Gruyere Cheese

Preheat oven to 350 degrees. Combine first 5 ingredients. Next beat eggs. Add to corn mixture. Add crackers, 1 cup of Am. Or Gruyere cheese, butter, salt and pepper. Mix well. Pour mixture into a well greased 2 qt. casserole. Make topping to spread on top of casserole. Mix 1 cup of grated cheese with sour cream and spread on top of casserole mixture. Sprinkle mixed chives.

Bake for 45 minutes to an hour.

Better Than Chips Roasted Potato Thins

1 large unpeeled baking potato

1/4 tsp. teaspoon salt

1/4 TBSP vegetable cooking spray

pinch white pepper

Heat oven to 400 degrees F. Cut potato into thin slices; arrange on an aluminum foil-lined backing pan. Lightly coat slices with cooking spray. Sprinkle with salt.

Bake for 30 minutes or until golden brown and crisp but not hard.

Note: Serve with a mixture of sour cream or yogurt chive dip.

Carrot Casserole for Your Eyes

- 1 lb. carrots cooked and drained
- 1 c. grated cheese
- ½ c. mayonnaise
- 1 crushed stick of Ritz 2 crackers
- 1 med. sauteed chopped onion (add green, yellow, or orange peppers)
- ¼ c. carrot juice

Heat oven to 350 degrees F. Mix all ingredients in a bowl. Spread mixture over carrots, Crush 1 stick of Ritz crackers and mix into carrots mixture. Salt and pepper to taste. It is optional if at this time you would like to add a ¼ teaspoon of curry spice. Put mixture in a square greased pan. Sprinkle Ritz crumbs and shredded cheese over top and cook for 25 minutes.

Note: Having a hard time getting someone to eat all of their carrots? Unless they are Bugs Bunny, dangling this root vegetable in front of them won't help but this casserole is a great way to introduce them to their new favorite vegetable, …the carrot.

Carrot Patties

3 large grated carrots

2 large eggs lightly beaten

2 stalks finely chopped celery

½ c. chopped Italian parsley

2 cloves grated garlic

¼ c. bread crumbs

1 large onion grated & onion juice has been squeezed out using a paper towel

1 tsp. coarse salt

¼ tsp. ground pepper

½ c. plain drained yogurt

Combine carrot, celery, onion, garlic, bread crumbs, eggs, parsley, salt and pepper. Form mixture into 2 inch patties. Brown patties at low heat in an oiled skillet for about 3 minutes per side. Remove from heat and drained oil from patties on a paper towel. Serve with a dollop of yogurt and parsley leaf.

Note: Kitchen Tips : Root vegetables should be smooth and firm. Very large carrots have woody cores, oversized radishes may be pithy, oversized turnips, beets, and parsnips may be woody. Fresh carrot tops usually mean fresh carrots, but condition of leaves on most other root vegetables does not indicate degree of freshness.

Deborah Odom

Sweet Potatoes Strudel

- 1 ½ lb. sweet potatoes, peeled and cut into 1/2 inch pieces (about 4 cups)
- ½ tsp. ground black pepper
- ¼ tsp. salt
- 1 large red onion, coarsely chopped
- (1 4 12x17-inch sheets frozen phyllo pastry, cup) thawed
- 5 TBSP olive oil
- 1 1/4 c. shredded parmesan cheese
- 2 cloves garlic, minced
- 1 tsp. snipped fresh parsley

Preheat the oven to 375 degrees F. In a medium mixed bowl, combine sweet potatoes, red onion, and 2 tbs of the olive oil, garlic, pepper, and salt. Toss to coat. Spread vegetables in a single layer in a shallow roasting pan. Roast, uncovered, about 40 minutes or until lightly browned and tender, stirring once. Set aside to cool for about 30 minutes. Increase the oven temperature to 425 degrees F. Unfold phyllo dough, cover with plastic wrap. Lay sheet of phyllo dough flat, brush with some of the remaining olive oil. Add 3 more sheets of phyllo, Brushing each sheet with olive oil. Add 1 cup parmesan cheese and savory to roasted vegetables mixture, toss to combine. Spread the vegetable mixture on top of the stacked sheet, leaving a 1-inch border on all sides. Fold the short sides in 1 inch over the filling, starting from a long side. Place the strudel, steam side down, on baking sheet. Brush the top and side of the strudel with olive oil. Sprinkle ¼ cup shredded parmesean cheese on top. Bake for 18 to 20 minutes or until browned. Cool on the baking sheet at least

15 minutes. Slice with a serrated knife and serve warm or at room temperature.

Note: This vegetable dish is so delicious that it could almost be considered a desert instead of a vegetable.

Deborah's Southern Baked Beans

1 large can of Bush's Baked Beans

1 large onion

1/2 or a large green bell pepper chopped

3 strips of finely chopped bacon

2 TBSP of butter

3 minced garlic cloves

1 TBSP of Lite Soy Sauce

1/4 to 1/2 cup of Barbeque Sauce or ketchup

1 TBSP of Maple Syrup

1/4 cup of Heavy Cream

In an iron skillet, over medium heat, sauté butter and bacon until tender and crisp. Next, add onion, bell pepper and garlic to the skillet and sauté until onions are translucent. Add baked beans and seasonings. Cover and simmer on very low heat, constantly stirring for about 20 - 30 minutes. Stir in the cream just before you serve the beans. Optional: Add cheese, leftover crumbled bite size meatloaf and serve over an onion roll or on lightly buttered and toasted French bread slices. YUMMY!

Miss Willadene's Fav's

Collards for Royalty

- 1 ½ pounds collards with stalks and large vein in the middle of the leaf removed
- ¼ tsp. ground pepper
- 1 cup diced onions
- 2 minced garlic cloves
- 2 quarts water
- 1 ham hock or substitute 2 cups of chicken stock
- 1 TBSP salt
- 1 TBSP sugar
- 2 cups small diced peeled white turnips

Wash collards three times in a basin of cold water. They are very sandy and each washing will allow the sand to drop to the bottom. Cut each leaf in half. Roll the leaves and cut into thin strips. In a 3 quart saucepan, place water and salt, sugar, and pepper. Add onions and garlic, and bring to a boil. (Sometimes I will add 1 bay leaf and then I will remove it before adding the ham hock.) Add ham hock or substitute 2 cups of chicken stock and simmer for 15 minutes. Add collard leaves and continue to simmer, cover set slightly ajar for 30 minutes. Add diced turnips and simmer, cover slightly ajar for an additional 30 minutes or until liquid is almost completely reduced.

Serve hot. GREAT with cornbread. *** If possible, try to buy the small collard leaves about 1 foot long.

Note: In the south, collards is a staple at the table. My mother and her family probably prepared collards at least 1-2 times a week. Some people do not like collards because they have never had a recipe where they were able to enjoy these woodsy vegetables. This recipe is so delicious that it will make a non collards eater ask the hostess for seconds.

Deborah Odom

Easy Halved Baked Potatoes

4 large russet potatoes, scrubbed

1/3 tsp. coarse salt

2 TBSP butter

1 dollop sour cream

4 sprigs fresh thyme

1/2 cup Grated Gruyere cheese

Heat oven to 425 degrees. Wash and dry potatoes. Pierce the skin with a fork and rub the outer-skins in the coarse salt. Slice the potatoes in half lengthwise, and arrange, cut sides up, in a baking dish. Next, Transfer baking dish to the oven on the lower rack, and bake until potatoes are golden brown and puffy on top, about 40 to 50 minutes. Serve each potato half topped with a dab of butter, sour cream, a fresh thyme sprig and salt and pepper to taste. Optional - sprinkle the top of the potatoes with your favorite finely shredded cheese.

Note: Kitchen Tip: Potatoes soaked in salt water for 20 minutes before baking will bake more rapidly.

Hawaiian Yams

3 Baked Mashed Sweet Potatoes

½ tsp. Salt

1 c. Sugar

1 Egg (beaten)

1 tsp. Vanilla

½ c. flaked Cocoanut

1 c. Milk

Heat oven to 350 degrees F. Thoroughly mix all ingredients and pour into buttered casserole dish. Bake 30 minutes. Spread on topping and return to oven for 5 min.

Topping: 1 large can crushed pineapple and juice, 1 cup sugar, 3 tbs cornstarch.

Combine and cook over medium-low heat stirring constantly until thick. Pour over potato mixture.

Deborah Odom

Holiday Favorite Green Bean Casserole

- 1 cup cream of mushroom soup
- 4 cup cooked can of green beans OR 1 lb. cooked fresh green beans
- ½ tsp. soy sauce
- dash pepper
- 1 cup French onions
- ½ cup whole milk
- 1 tsp. molasses

Heat oven to 350 degrees F. In a 1 ½ qt casserole combine soup, milk, soy, molasses, and pepper. Stir in bean and ½ can of onions. Bake for 25 minutes. Top with remaining onions. Bake for 5 minutes.

Note: We always had Sunday night suppers at church, just before the service began. So, everyone brought their special recipes and it was a given that they always wanted mother to bring this casserole. Mothers recipe is soooo good because it does not have that aftertaste that some of the bean casseroles have.

Mac & Cheeses

7 TBSP butter

½ tsp. minced garlic

4 TBSP bechamel sauce

1 c. grated cheddar cheese

2 cups half & half

1 c. fontina

¾ tsp. salt

1 c. grated gruyere cheese

¼ tsp. fresh grated pepper

¼ c. bread crumbs

2 cups grated parmesan-reggiano cheese pinch chopped parsley or dried parsley

1 lb. elbow Macaroni

Preheat oven to 350 degrees F. Use 1 tbs of butter to grease a 3 casserole dish. Cook pasta according to directions on the package. Prepare bechamel sauce: in a heavy, medium saucepan, melt 4 tbs of butter over low heat. Add the flour and stir to combine. Cook stirring constantly for about 3 minutes. Increase the heat to medium & whisk in the half & half little by little. Sit frequently and cook until thickened about 4 to 5 minutes. Remove from heat, Season with salt and pepper and stir in 1 cup of parmesan cheese until cheese is melted. Place a lid to keep warm. Drain the cooked pasta. In a large bowl, combine the pasta and 2 tbs of butter and garlic, Next, stir in the bechamel sauce. In a separate bowl, combine all 4 chesses so that you can layer your casserole dish. Now begin an assembly line of layering the 4 chesses with the macaroni bechamel sauce, Finally, combine bread crumbs and 1 oz of grated parmigiana and parsley and sprinkle over casserole. Bake 40-45 minutes.

Deborah Odom

Note: We enjoy eating this vegetarian meal with a garden salad, fresh homemade chicken soup, and crispy garlic bread rounds. And for desert? Apple turnovers.

Mid-Eastern Baked Rice

2 c. Basmati Rice

1 tsp. of salt

1 stick butter

1/2 pkg. thawed lima beans

1 tsp. Crisco oil

Boil rice and lima beans in water. In the bottom of a skillet, heat oil. and add boiled rice. Place 1 stick of sliced butter on top of rice and lima beans. Heat rice over low heat until butter has melted. Salt and pepper to taste.

Note: This recipe was shared by a precious neighbor who was from the royal house in Iran. The taste is fabulous.

Deborah Odom

Sauteed Spinach

½ c. golden raisins

2 cloves garlic thinly sliced

¼ c. finely chopped onions

¼ c. toasted pine nuts

1 TBSP olive oil

2 bunches about 2 lbs. of washed baby fresh spinach with large stems or veins removed

Coarse salt and fresh ground pepper

1 TBSP sugar

In a bowl, add raisins and cover with ¾ of warm water. In a 6 qt saucepan, heat olive oil. Stir in onions and garlic and saute for 1 minute. Add nuts and cook for about one minute or until golden brown. Drain raisins and add them to pan with the spinach.

Flavor with salt and pepper and sugar to taste. Cook an additional 3-5 minutes.

Note: For creamed spinach, add ¼ cup of heavy whipping cream to the above mixture. Pulse in a food processor until the mixture is creamy. Do not sprinkle the pine nuts on top until the end. Serve right away. Immediately refrigerate any left over's.

Shoepeg Corn Casserole

¼ c. canned milk

1 dash lite soy sauce

½ stick margarine

1 dash fresh ground pepper

(6-oz.) cream cheese

Sprinkle of dried parsley

2 boxes shoe peg corn or 1 bag shoe peg corn

Heat oven to 325 degrees F. Cook milk, margarine, and cream cheese over medium heat. Then add shoe peg corn, soy sauce, and pepper. Place in a buttered casserole 13 X 9 X 2 casserole dish and sprinkle the top with parsley. Bake for 30 minutes.

Deborah Odom

Skillet Potatoes with Herbs

6 TBSP butter

1 cup grated parmesan or American sharp

1/2 tsp. salt cheese

1/2 TBSP basil leaves

1/4 tsp. ground pepper

1 sliced large onion

1 cup heavy whipping cream

1/4 tsp. thyme leaves

1 slice of white bread pulsed in food processor for toppin

2 lbs. potatoes peeled very thinly sliced

Preheat oven to 425 degrees. Combine seasonings in bowl. Place 2 tbs butter in 10 inch skillet. Arrange a think layer of potatoes, onions and cheese slices in a circular pattern in skillet. Sprinkle thyme, salt and pepper. Pour cream on top. Bake for 20 minutes. Uncover and bake for 20 minutes. Remove from oven. Press layers down.

Sprinkle with grated cheese and bread topping.

Note: For generations, mothers family have ALWAYS had guests at the table. They might have been a cherished relative, the visiting preacher, the encumbered judge, or even the president..Yes, I said the president even ate at their table! This was a delicious vegetable that could serve many people or for a small crowd,there would be enough for seconds

Southern Crumb Dressing

2 cups fresh white bread crumbs

½ cup finely minced sauteed onions

2 cups cooked crumbled cornbread

¼ tsp. celery salt

1/3 tsp. ground sage

2 cups rich chicken stock

½ tsp. salt

1 tsp. sugar

½ tsp. pepper

Pre heat oven to 350° Mix all ingredients together and place in a glass casserole dish.

Bake for about 35 minutes. Keep your eye on the oven and watch carefully to be sure that the dressing does not dry out. Mixture should be moist - not wet.

Note: This is the dressing that the northerners wonder how the southerners make and the southerners wonder why the northerners do not know how!

Deborah Odom

Squash Casserole

2 lb. boiled squash sliced or 1 qt fresh or frozen or 1 lb can of squash

2 grated carrots

1 c. of cream of chicken soup

1 (2-oz.) jar chopped pimento

1 c. sour cream

2 TBSP grated onion

1 stick butter

Combine squash, pimento, onion, and carrots. Mix well. Combine undiluted soup and sour cream and stir into vegetables mixture. Toss together casserole dish. Pour vegetables mixture over all and top with remaining stuffing. Bake at 375 degrees covered for 30 minutes. Option: grate 1 cup of cheese over top of casserole.

Steamed Cabbage

1 leafy green head of cabbage   2 Tbs butter

2 Tbs canola oil   dash lite soy sauce

Cut cabbage in half and core. Lay flat sides on cutting board. Cut into thin slices. Drop into cold water until ready to cook. Melt 2 tablespoons of butter in heavy pot (like soup pot). Add 2 tablespoons canola oil. Use large fork to lift cabbage out of water into butter mixture. Let water drip from cabbage. Cover. Cook on low heat several minutes. There will be enough to make steam. Use fork to turn cabbage over.

Cook until tender. Season with soy sauce to taste.

Note: Kitchen Tips : When cooking cabbage, place a small tin cup or can half full of vinegar on the stove near the cabbage, and it will absorb all of the odor from it.

Stuffed Squash

- 2 TBSP finely chopped onions
- 3 TBSP bread crumbs
- 1 tsp. chopped parsley
- 1 hard boiled egg chopped fine
- 2 TBSP butter
- 1 tsp. chopped pimento
- 1 cup squash pulp, seeds and skin chopped fine
- Salt and pepper
- 12 small to medium yellow squash

Cook unpeeled squash in boiling salted water until tender. Cool. Cut the squash in half length wise and scoop out the centers with a teaspoon and reserve. Saute onion and parsley in butter until onion is yellow and soft. Add squash pulp, 2 tablespoons bread crumbs, egg and pimento. Mix and season to your taste with salt and pepper.

Fill cavities of the squash and sprinkle with 1 tablespoon of bread crumbs, buttered.

Place squash on a buttered tray and bake at 350 degrees for 20 minutes.

Note: At Thanksgiving, Mother made a beautiful table when she presented these vibrant yellow vegetable plated on a white, lacy, oblong, china platter. She would prepare at least 8 squash, but it was enough for 16 people or for 8 people to have seconds.

Miss Willadene's Fav's

Sweet Potato Casserole

6 med. sweet potatoes or canned yams

1 tsp. vanilla

1 cup granulated sugar

1 cup brown sugar

2 sticks butter

¼ cup flour

2 eggs beaten

1 cup pecans, chopped

Heat oven to 350 degrees F. Cook and mash potatoes. Cool, then add granulated sugar, ½ stick butter eggs, vanilla and milk. Put into casserole dish. For topping, mix flour, brown sugar, and nuts, Then add unsalted butter. Spread on top of potatoes.

Bake uncovered for 1 hour (I always check after 45 minutes).

Note: Kitchen Tip: Puerto Rico and Nancy Hall varieties of sweet potatoes, with bronze to rosy skins are soft and sweet when cooked. Yellow to light brown potatoes are the jersey types that are firmer and less moist.

Deborah Odom

Traditional Cornbread Dressing

½ cup chopped onion

1 TBSP dried sage

1 cup chopped celery

½ TBSP black pepper

1/3 cup butter or margarine

3 cups chicken broth

6 cups of crumbled, cooked Martha white cornbread

2 eggs, beaten

dash of lite soy sauce

4 -2 ½ cup slices bread, torn into small pieces

Heat oven to 450° F. Grease 13x9-X 2 inch baking dish or pan. In small skillet, cook and stir onion and celery in butter until tender. In large bowl, combine cooked celery mixture, cornbread, bread, sage and black pepper; and soy sauce. Add broth and eggs to cornbread mixture; mix well. Pour into greased baking dish and bake for 30 minutes or until golden brown. FOR A VARIATION: Omit sage and cook 2 cups chopped red bell pepper with onions; add to cornbread mixture. Substitute green chilies for pepper. Bake as directed.

Miss Willadene's Fav's

Uncle Dan's Hopin Johns

- 2 cups of freshly shelled or frozen black-eyed peas or crowther peas.
- 4 cups of chicken stock
- 1 whole onion chopped
- 2 cloves of minced garlic
- 4 slices of finely chopped bacon
- 1/2 cup of chopped bell peppers red or green
- 1 tsp of salt
- 1 tsp of pepper
- 1 TBSP of Molasses
- 1/2 tsp of salt
- 1/4 cup of heavy cream

On medium to low heat, sauté bacon until slightly crisp. Add onion, garlic and bell pepper. Next, add fresh or frozen peas. Add 4 cups of chicken stock. Add salt and pepper and Molasses. Bring to a boil. Simmer on low heat for 45 to 50 minutes until peas are tender. Stir in cream. As needed, add more seasonings for taste.

Vegetable Casserole

1 lg pkg mixed vegetable

1 c. chopped celery

1 c. grated cheese

1 red onion chopped

1 c. mayo

1 tube of Ritz crackers crumbled

Heat oven at 350 degrees F. Cook vegetables. Mix with all ingredients. Butter a 8 X 8 casserole dish and place vegetables in it. If vegetable mixture is too thick, add tablespoons of cooked vegetable broth from your cooked vegetables until you reach your desired consistency. The casserole should not dry out. It should be moist. Finally, sprinkle with crumbled crackers cheese. Cook for 25 minutes.

Note: Kitchen Tip :If you add a little milk to water in which cauliflower is cooking, the cauliflower will remain attractively white.

Miss Willadene's Fav's

Deborah Odom

BREADS & ROLLS

Deborah Odom

TIPS FOR BREAD

❈ For lighter biscuits, rolls or muffins, heat greased pan, tin or baking sheet for a few minutes before pouring in the batter.

❈ Test the water for yeast by feeling if the water is very warm on the inside of your wrist.

❈ If you can't find a draft free place to let dough rise, then heat the oven to 200 degrees for 5 minutes and then turn the oven off. Place dough inside and close the door.

❈ Always knead the dough towards you and with the palm of your hand.

❈ Cover the yeast dough for buns and cakes with a greased plastic wrap. This will prevent skim from forming on the dough.

❈ If you want to see if your bread dough has doubled in bulk, insert your fingers a half of an inch into the dough. If the dent remains, the dough is ready to be punched down.

❈ The yeast bread is done if the loaf sounds hollow when the crust is tapped.

❈ Sinking fruit and nuts in bread batter can be prevented if you heat the fruit or nuts and dust in flour before adding it to the dough.

❈ Stale bread can turn into croutons. Cut crust removed stale bread into slices, then cubes. Next, bake at 325 degrees for 15 20 minutes. Check and stir throughout the cooking time.

❈ Greasy doughnut taste can be eliminated if you add a small amount of vinegar to the deep fat while frying the doughnuts.

❈ Restore brown sugar by placing sugar in an airtight container with a piece of apple or a slice of bread.

A Recipe For A Happy Day

1 cup of Friendly Words

A dash of Humor

2 heaping cups of Understanding

4 heaping tsp's. of Time and Patience

A pinch of a Warm Personality

A cupful of Loving Tenderness

All day long, measure your words carefully;

add heaping cups of understanding,

Use generous amounts of time, and patience.

Keep the flame burning by adding cupfuls of warm loving tenderness.

Add a dash of humor, and a pinch of personality.

Season to taste with the spices of life.

Serve in individual molds.

Deborah Odom

Banana Bread

2/3 cups Crisco (not liquid)
2 cups sifted flour
1 cup Sugar
1 1/2 tsp. baking soda

1 cup mashed ripe bananas
1/2 tsp. salt
1 tsp. lemon juice
2 eggs

Heat oven to 375 degrees F. Cream Crisco and sugar. Beat eggs until light and add mashed bananas and lemon juice. Sift flour, baking soda, and salt together. Add flour mixture to banana mixture. Stir until mixed. Pour in a loaf pan and bake for 35 to 45 minutes.

Banana Muffins

1/2 c. butter

1 tsp. nutmeg

1 c. sugar

1 tsp. baking soda

2 eggs

2 tsp. hot water

1 c. mashed bananas

1 tsp. vanilla

1 1/2 c. sifted flour

Cream butter and sugar. Add eggs and bananas. Mix well. Stir in flour and nutmeg. Dissolve baking soda in hot water. Add to banana mixture. Stir vanilla. Fill grease muffin tins {or paper baking cups} about half full. Bake at 350 for 20 minutes or until golden brown.

Note: Dip your bananas in lemon juice right after they are peeled. They will not turn dark and the faint flavor of lemon really adds quite a bit. The same may be done with apples.

Deborah Odom

Best Ever Spoon Bread

3 cups whole milk

2 TBSP Butter

1 1/4 cups plain cornmeal

1 3/4 TBSP baking powder

3 large eggs

1 tsp. salt

Preheat oven at 375 degrees. Stir meal into rapidly boiling milk. Cook until very thick, stirring constantly to prevent scorching. Remove from burner and allow to cool. The mixture will be cold and very stiff. Add well beaten egg, salt, baking powder and melted butter. Beat with electric beater for 15 minutes. If hand beating is used break the hardened cooked meal into the beaten eggs in small amounts until all is well mixed. Then beat thoroughly for 10 minutes using a wooden spoon. Pour into 2 well greased casseroles. Bake for 30 minutes.

Cheesy Onion Bread

1/2 tsp. onion powder

3/4 c. finely diced onion

1/2 c. whole milk

1 TBSP chopped fresh chives or parsley leaves

1 egg beaten

1 1/2 c. biscuit mix

1/4 tsp. salt

1 c. shredded sharp cheddar

4 TBSP melted butter

Preheat the oven to 400 degrees. Heat 2 TBSP butter in a small skillet over medium heat. Add the onions and cook until tender. Mix the milk and egg into the biscuit mix, stirring just until the mix is moistened. Fold in the onions and ½ cup of the cheese. Spoon mixture into a greased 8 inch round cake pan. Mix the onion powder and salt into 2 TBSP of melted butter and drizzle the mixture over the dough. Sprinkle the break with chives or parsley and bake for 15 minutes. Next sprinkle remaining ½ cup cheese and bake until the bread is cooked, about 5 minutes longer.

Deborah Odom

Cheesy Puff Pastry Twist

1 {17.3 oz } pkg. frozen puff pastry sheets ,thawed

1/4 tsp. garlic powder

1/4 c. melted butter

1 c. freshly grated parmesan

1/8 tsp. white pepper

1 tsp. dried basil

1/2 tsp kosher salt

Preheat oven to 400 degrees. Lightly grease a baking sheet. On a lightly floured surface, unfold pastry sheets. Cut each sheet into strips, about ¾ by 10- inches a piece. In a shallow dish, combine cheese, basil, salt, pepper and garlic. Brush pastry sticks with melted butter. Roll pastry in cheese mixture, lightly coating each side. Gently twist pastry sticks,and place on a prepared baking sheet. Bake for 12 minutes. Remove to wire racks to cool.

Cinnamon Rolls

1/4 c. warm/hot water

1pkg. quick action dry yeast

3/4 c. lukewarm milk

1/4 c. sugar

1 tsp. salt

2 1/4 cubes soft butter (room temp.)

3 1/2 to 3 3/4 c. flour

1 egg (room temp.)

cinnamon

brown sugar

Optional: nuts and raisins

Frosting:

3c. powdered sugar

2-3 TBSP butter

1-2 tsp. vanilla

2 TBSP milk

Rising Temperature: 200 degrees. Baking Temperature: 350 degrees. Put ¼ cup of warm/hot water in warm large plastic bowl. Add quick action dry yeast. Sprinkle ¼ cup sugar over yeast, let sit 5 to 10 minutes until foamy and bubbly (discard and start over if yeast does not foam or bubble). Add a couple of the cups of flour along with the one cube of butter and mix more flour and continuously beat by hand. Add egg and continue to add flour until all flour is used. Knead dough into a ball and place dough in a big pot and cover with moist towel. Place pot in pre-warmed 200° oven and turn the oven off. Let rise for one hour or until double size (time varies by climate). Lightly flour counter and knead dough to 1/3" to ½" thickness. Pat butter over all dough and sprinkle with cinnamon and brown sugar (add optional nuts and or raisins) to taste. Roll into jelly roll and cut into 1 ½" to 2" pieces. Place rolls (slightly touching, allowing room for them to rise) in baking pan. Put in pre-warmed 200° oven and turn the oven off. Place a mug of water or a moist towel in the oven, but not on the rolls. Let rise ½ hour. Cook 350° for 12 minutes, then watch until done to your taste. FROSTING: beat ingredients until creamy. More milk will create a glaze, less will create a thick frosting. Vary by reducing sugar and substituting 4 to 8 ounces of cream cheese.

Coffee Cake

1 3/4 c. sugar	4 egg whites
3/4 c. butter	Topping:
1 1/8 c. milk	1 1/8 c. brown sugar
3 c. flour sifted	2 TBSP cinnamon
4 tsp. baking powder	3/4 c. flour
1 tsp. salt	3/4 butter

Cream sugar & butter until soft & smooth. Add milk alternately with flour & baking powder & salt sifted together. Fold in egg whites beaten stiff. Pour into buttered baking pan. Cover with topping. Topping: Combine crumble ingredients with a fork. Spread on top & bake at 350 degrees 40 to 50 minutes.

Doughnuts

4 tsp. baking powder	sugar and cinnamon
1 tsp. salt	3 1/2 c. flour
1 egg and 2 egg yolks	1 c. milk
1 c. sugar	3 TBSP melted butter

Sift dry ingredients. Beat the eggs, add milk, sugar and cooled melted butter. Add the dry ingredients to form a soft dough. Roll out on floured board, knead and roll out ¼" thick. Cut and fry in deep fat at 370 degrees. Turn once. Remove. Roll in sugar

Everyday Bran Muffins

1 (15 oz.) box Raisin Bran	3 tsp. baking powder
3 c. sugar	5 c. flour
2 tsp. salt	2 tsp. baking soda
1 tsp. pumpkin pie spice mix	2 tsp. vanilla
4 beaten eggs	2 sticks butter (melted)
1 qt. butter milk	

Beat eggs, vanilla, butter and buttermilk. Add dry ingredients. Blend/ mix well. Bake 15 to 20 minutes. May keep the batter for 5 weeks in fridge.

Deborah Odom

Generational Quick Whipping Cream Biscuits

1/2 c. butter

2 c. self-rising flour

3/4 to 1 c. whipping cream

1/4 c. butter melted

Heat oven to 400 degrees F. Cut: ½ cup butter into flour with a pastry blender or fork until crumbly. Add whipping cream, stirring just until dry and ingredients are moistened. Turn: dough out onto a lightly floured surface, and knead lightly 3 or 4 times. Roll or pat dough ¾-inch thickness. Cut with a 2-inch round cutter;place biscuits on a lightly greased baking sheet Bake: for 13 to 15 minutes. Brush biscuits with ¼ cup melted butter. Variation: ¾ cup buttermilk and 1 tablespoons granulated sugar, stirred together, may be substituted for whipping cream.

Note: This recipe is from my great, great, great grandmother. It is so good that they brought a bagged lunch of biscuits with them when they came over on the Mayflower.

Hot Biscuits

2 c. flour sifted

3tsp. baking powder

1 tsp. salt

1/3 c. shortening

3/4 c. milk

Sift flour, baking powder, salt together. Cut in shortening until mixture resembles coarse cornmeal. Turn on lightly floured board. Knead lightly. Roll or pat ½ inch thick. Cut with biscuit place on ungreased cookie sheet. Bake in hot 450 degrees 12 to 15 minutes.

Note: Kneading the dough for a half minute after mixing improves the texture of baking powder biscuits.

Deborah Odom

Hot Rolls

3 TBSP sugar

1 cup lukewarm water

1 tsp. salt 1 pkg. Red Star yeast dissolved in 1/4 cup warm water

1 egg

3 TBSP Wesson oil

4 cups flour

Mix sugar and salt. Add egg and beat well. Add oil and lukewarm water. Stir well and mix in flour. Put in clean, greased bowl in warm place and let rise until double in bulk. Pour out on floured surface and work down, Then let dough lie for five minutes. Make into rolls. Let rise again, then bake until golden brown. Bake oven temperature 400.

Iris Nut Roll

1 box vanilla wafers (crushed)

2 c. chopped pecans.

1 c. sweetened condensed milk

1/2 c. chopped candy cherries.

Mix with hands. Roll into a log or logs and freeze. When frozen, slice thin roll in confectionate sugar. NO BAKE.

Paper Thin Lacy Corn Cakes

- 1 cup Yellow corn meal - plain
- 1 1/3 cup whole milk
- 1/3 cup all - purpose - plain flour
- 2 large Egg Whites
- 1/2 tsp. Salt
- 2 tsp. Vegetable oil
- 1/2 tsp. Sugar
- 1/2 c. Frozen Corn Kernels, Thawed, Drained, and Cooked
- 1/8 tsp. Baking Soda

In a large bowl, combine the cornmeal, flour, salt, sugar and baking soda. Stir to mix.

In a separate container, combine the milk, egg whites and oil. Stir the liquid ingredients into the dry ingredients with a few quick strokes. Heat the corn kernels in the microwave for about 3-5 minutes. COOL. Then, stir in the corn kernels. Allow to stand 10 min. to thicken slightly. Lightly coat a griddle or nonstick skillet with nonstick spray. Pour about ¼ cup of batter or less per cake. Cook over medium to medium-high heat until small bubbles form on top of each cake, then turn over and cook about 30 seconds on the other side. Keep warm in a low oven. If the cakes are to thick, add water to thin the batter. The cakes should look like lace cookies and be crispy -not like the looks or consistency of pancakes.

Note: DELICIOUS! You may have to triple this recipe. Whenever my great grandmother, grandmother, mother, or myself would make these crispy treats at family dinners, the men of the family could never eat just one.

Pop Overs

1 c. sifted all purpose flour   1/4 tsp. salt

2 eggs   1 TBSP melted butter

Pre heat oven at 450 degrees. Mix the flour and salt. Beat eggs until light, add milk and butter and add slowly to the flour. Stir until well blended. Beat 1 minute with electric beater. Heavily butter muffin tins and put in the oven to get hot. Fill the cups one third. Bake 20 minutes at 450 degrees, then reduce heat to 350 degrees and bake 15 minutes more. Don't peek!

Pumpkin Pecan Bread

1/2 c. soften butter

1 tsp. baking soda

2 c. sugar

2 tsp. salt

4 eggs

1 tsp. nutmeg

1 can (16 oz) solid pack pumpkin

2 c. chopped pecans

1 c. milk

1 c. golden raisins

4 c. sifted flour

cream cheese spread

4 tsp. baking powder

Preheat oven to 350 degrees. Combine butter and sugar in a large bowl and beat until light and fluffy. Beat in eggs, pumpkin, and milk. Sift together flour, baking power, baking soda, salt, cinnamon, and nutmeg. Add to pumpkin mixture and stir until thoroughly mixed. Stir in pecans and raisins. Speard evenly in 2 well- greased 9x5x3 loaf pans. Bake at 350 degrees for 50 to 60 mintues or until wooden pick inserted in center and comes out clean. Cool in pan on wire rack for 5 minutes:remove from pan and cool completely on rack. Serve with cream cheese spread.

Deborah Odom

Scones

2 c. sifted flour	4 TBSP butter
2 eggs	1/2 c. heavy cream
1/2 tsp. salt	2 tsp. sugar
4 tsp. Baking. powder	

Mix dry ingredients work in butter. Add well beaten eggs. Cream together add cream. Put on floured board ¾" thick. Cut in diamond shape. Brush end with unbeaten egg white mixed with water. Bake 450 degrees 15 minutes. Sprinkle with powdered sugar.

Miss Willadene's Fav's

Scrumptious Scones

2 1/2 cups all-purpose flour

3 TBSP butter cut into bits and chilled

1 tsp. double acting baking powder

1 egg beaten to a froth

1/4 cup granulated sugar

1/2 cup whole milk

1/2 tsp. salt

Preheat oven to 400°. It is very important to begin the next part of the recipe with a chilled bowl. Mix together flour, baking powder, 1 tablespoon of sugar, salt and butter. Using your fingertips, rub until mixture looks like coarse meal. Reserve 1 tablespoon of frothy egg and combine the remainder of egg with milk and add to flour mixture. Using a fork, mix until the dough forms a ball. Place dough between floured sides of wax paper and roll to ¼ ' thickness. Cut into round squares and arrange on a baking sheet placing the rounds 1' apart from each other. Next coat tops of rounds with reserved egg, sprinkle with remaining sugar. Bake in the middle of oven until light brown about 15 minutes. Makes about 10-12 scones

Deborah Odom

Spoon Bread

2 c. milk

1/2 tsp. sugar

1/2 c. cornmeal

2 tsp. melted butter

1 TBSP salt

3 eggs separated

1/2 tsp. baking powder

Heat oven to 315 degrees F. Scald milk, and add cornmeal. Cook until thick. Add salt baking powder, sugar, and butter. Beat egg yokes and add to corn mixture. Beat the egg whites to a soft peak and fold in batter. Pour batter into a well buttered 1 ½ qt. pan. Bake for 25 to 30 minutes.

Miss Willadene's Fav's

Deborah Odom

DESSERTS

TIPS FOR DESERTS

* Adding 1 teaspoon of lemon juice to the batter when creaming butter and sugar of cake recipe that uses butter and sugar will improve the taste to the cake batter.

* Freeze cakes and cookies in freezer bags.

* Quick cake flour: Place 2 tablespoons of cornstarch in a 1 cup measuring cup. Fill cup with all purpose flour and sift 3 times. This mixture is equal to 1 cup of sifted cake flour.

* Cracked sugar icing? Add pinch of baking powder to powdered sugar icings to prevent hardening and cracking in icings.

* Use a large kitchen salt shaker to dust flour onto pans.

* Stale Cake? Place a cut apple in cake container to restore moisture in cake.

* Flakier pie crust? Add 1 teaspoon of vinegar to cold water in pie pastry.

* Quick perfect pie dough: Mix 3 pounds of flour, 2 pounds of solid Crisco or lard, 2 tablespoons of sugar and 2 tablespoons of salt together until mixture has a coarse consistency. Divide dough into 6 equal parts and store in freezer bags. When ready to use, add ice water until mixture is moistened. Roll out. Make enough pie dough for 3 double-crust pies.

* Golden crust pie? Brush with milk just before baking pie.

* For golden puffy crust, brush with egg whites.

* Before baking, prick pie shell thoroughly with a fork to deep the pie shell from bubbling up.

* Sprinkle salt over your pastry board before wiping it.

* FREEZING PIE SHELLS: Uncooked pie shells can be kept for 2 months in the freezer and baked pie shells can be kept for up to 4 months. Baked fruit pies will keep 4 months and chiffon pies will keep for 1 month. Custards, meringue and cream pies cannot be frozen.

* Angel food cakes, chiffon cakes and sponge cakes should be baked in ungreased pans.

* Bake foam cakes in the bottom rack of your oven

Miss Willadene's Fav's

❊ Foam cakes are done when the cracks in the top of the cake feel dry.

❊ Unfrosted cakes can be kept in the freezer for up to 4 months. Frosted cakes will keep half that time.

Deborah Odom

A generational favorite - Butter Nut Cake

- 1 cup of shortening
- 2 cups of sugar
- 4 eggs
- 2 1/2 cups of sifted cake flour
- 1/2 cup of self rising flour
- 1 cup of sweet milk
- 1-2 tsps of butternut flavor
- 2 oz. jar of chopped pimento
- 1 cup of milk
- 2 eggs well beaten
- 1 cup of finely crushed cracker crumbs
- 2 cups of grated American or Gruyere cheese
- 1/2 cup of melted butter
- 1/4 tsp of salt
- 1/4 tsp of pepper
- 1 8 Oz. carton of sour cream
- Minced chives for garnishing

Preheat oven to 350 degrees. Cream shortening, and sugar, for 10 minutes. Add eggs. Beat well. Add 1 cup of flour and beat at slow speed for 1 minute. Add remaining flour and milk alternately. Beat until well mixed. Add salt and butternut flavoring. COOL completely before frosting cake.

Miss Willadene's Fav's

Frosting

1 8 oz. pkg. of softened cream cheese

1 stick of softened butter

1 box of white Confectioner Sugar

1/4 tsp of Salt

2 cups of chopped pecans

1 - 2 TBSPS of Butternut flavoring

Cream first 2 ingredients together. Slowly add sugar, salt and flavoring. If frosting is too thick, add tablespoons of milk to form spreading consistency. Sprinkle chopped pecans on sides and top of cake.

5 Generation Wilson's Chess Pie Bars

1 Duncan Hines yellow mix (no butter)

4 eggs

1 box powdered sugar-white

1 (8-oz.) pkg. cream cheese

1 stick butter

2 c. pecans chopped

Mix 1 stick of butter with one egg and cake. Mix together. Put into bowl and work it into a ball. Press into a greased pan. Press pecans hard in pan. Filling: Stir cream cheese, sugar and 3 eggs until smooth. Pour over pecans. Bake at 300 degrees for 1 to 1 hour and 15 minutes. Check the pie for doneness. Let it cool. Cut into bars; dip the knife in water after each cut.

Note: Lazy summer days were great with these chess bars. I enjoyed them when my great grandmother fixed them for me, and so did she when her grandmother fixed them for her. The only difference is that I substituted a Cake mix where as my great grandmothers grandmother, made the cake batter from scratch. Either way, they are scrumptious.

A Desert for the Living

1 c. love

1/2 lb. pride, cut into small portions

1/4 c. will power packed firm

1 lb. humility

(3-oz.) determination

sprinkle common sense

dash of flexibility

1 large head understanding

1 (8-oz.) can foresight

a hint of hindsight

few leaves of awareness (fresh, if possible)

few springs of humor

seasoned to taste

pinch of adventure

Saute love and understanding until tender. Mix well and continue cooking gently. In a large bowl, blend will power and determination well to avoid procrastination adding a dash of flexibility to accommodate life's delicate variations. Fold in a few leaves of awareness (more, if you savor knowledge). Set aside to rise and expand its flavor throughout the day. In a separate bowl, combine pride, whisked lightly with humility.

Pour in common sense and sprinkle lightly with adventure. Set oven with foresight for each new day. But hindsight...just enough to profit from the old. Season entire mixture with humor. Bake for 24 hours. Testing often and adjusting to the wonders of each day.

Deborah Odom

Apple Cake

1/2 c. Wesson Oil

1 tsp. soda

3 c. cake flour

2 tsp. vanilla

1 tsp. salt

1 c. cut pecans

3 well beaten eggs

3 c. cooking apples

1 tsp. cinnamon

Heat oven to 350 degrees F. Sift flour, salt, cinnamon, soda, and sugar together. Add eggs, oil, and vanilla. Next apples and nuts. Bake in a tube pan for 1 hour and 15 min.

Then add frosting. Frosting: 1 stick of butter, a can coconut, 1 cup pecans, 1 cup brown sugar, 1 egg. Cook all ingredients in double boiler until thick. Cool and frost cake.

Note: After a cake comes from the oven, it should be placed on a rack for about five minutes. Then the sides should be loosened and the cake turned out on rack to finish cooling.

Miss Willadene's Fav's

Aunt Willa's Eclair Cake

1 box plain graham crackers

1 1/2 c. confectioner sugar

2 (3 1/4-oz.) boxes instant French vanilla pudding

2 squares of cooled melted unsweetened chocolate

3 1/2 c. milk

3 TBSP of softened butter

(1-8 oz.) container of frozen whipped topping thawed

1/3 c. milk

2 tsp. light corn-syrup

Frosting: 2 tsp. pure vanilla extract

Butter a 13 x 9 x 2 pan, put a whole graham cracker layer in dish. Use an electric mixer, mix pudding with 3 ½ cups of milk and beat for 2 min. at medium speed. Fold in whipped topping and pour ½ pudding over graham crackers. Layer g. c another layer of pudding and end with graham crackers and spread chocolate frosting on top.

FROSTING: Blend sugar and squares. Add butter and milk, add corn-syrup and vanilla, frost and refrigerate for 24 hours.

Note: Chancellor is a charming little town on highway 52, in Alabama. This town has the BEST peach and pear orchards, pecan trees, barbeque and the BEST cook in the town, Great Aunt Willa! She is a true southern lady, full of composure and lady like charm. She sent this recipe to my mother and we just love it.

Deborah Odom

Award Winning Brownie Cake

- 1/2 pound butter, softened at room temperature
- 4 TBSP cocoa powder
- 1/2 tsp. salt
- 2 cups all-purpose flour
- 1/2 cup buttermilk
- 2 eggs
- 1/2 cup sour cream
- 2 cups sugar
- 1 tsp. vanilla extract
- 1 tsp. baking soda
- 2 tsp. brewed or instant coffee

Preheat the oven to 350 degrees F. Grease and flour 2(9-inch) cake pans, then line with parchment paper. In the bowl using an electric mixer, cream butter and sugar until light and fluffy. Beat in the eggs one at a time. Add the cooled coffee. Into a medium mixing bowl, sift the flour, baking soda and cocoa powder and salt together.

In a small mixing bowl whisk the buttermilk, sour cream and vanilla together. While the mixer is on low speed, add the dry ingredients in 3 batches, alternating with the liquid ingredients. If you end with the dry ingredients, the cake will be tough. Evenly pour the cake batter into 2 greased 9 inch cake pans lined with waxed paper. Bake for about 30 minutes. Remove cakes from cake pan and let cool on wire racks for about an hour or until cool to the touch. Frost with Award Winning Frosting to follow.

Note: If you are a chocolate lover, this will hit the spot. This dish was a favorite amongst the children at the annual family reunions on the grounds in Alabama.

Award Winning Chocolate Buttermilk Frosting

1 stick butter, softened

2 Tbs buttermilk

4 squares Unsweetened chocolate

1 tsp. vanilla

8 oz. cream cheese

1/4 tsp. salt

1 pound powdered sugar, sifted

In the microwave, melt butter and 2 squares of unsweetened chocolate. Cool. In a bowl using an electric mixer, combine the butter, chocolate, salt, and cream cheese over low speed and mix until thoroughly combined. Increase speed to high and cream ingredients until and fluffy. Reduce speed to low and slowly add the powdered sugar, buttermilk, and vanilla. Beat until mixture is smooth and thoroughly combined.

Deborah Odom

Banana Pudding

5-6 sliced Bananas

1/3 c. Flour

4 Eggs Separated

2 c. Milk

1 box Vanilla Wafers

1 Tbs Vanilla Extract

3/4 c. Sugar

Dash of Salt

Combine ½ c. of sugar, flour and salt, in double boiler. Stir in 4 egg yolks and milk. Blend well, cook stirring over boiled water. Until thickened. Next reduce heat to about low to medium. Stirring for about 5 minutes. Remove from heat, should be like a pudding consistency. Layer a casserole dish with pudding, wafer bananas, wafer, bananas, and last pudding. Beat egg whites stiff. Gradually add ¼ cup sugar and beat stiff. Add vanilla. Bake at 425° for 5 minutes.

Banana - Pecan Cake

4 TBSP butter, room temp. plus more for pan

1/4 c. butter milk

1/2 tsp. pure vanilla extract

1 c. sifted cake flour (not self-rising) plus more for pan

1/3 c. firmly packed dark-brown sugar

1 large egg

1/4 tsp. salt

1/2 tsp. baking soda

1/3 c. chopped toasted pecans

1/4 tsp. each baking powder, salt, and ground cinnamon

confectioner's sugar for dusting

pinch of ground cloves

sweetened whipped

1 very ripe large banana, mashed (about 1/2 cup)

Preheat oven to 350 degrees. Butter a 6-by-2-inch round cake pan. Line bottom with parchment paper, butter and dust with flour. Set aside. Into bowl, sift flour, Baking soda, baking powder, salt and vanilla. In a large bowl, cream butter and brown sugar until light and fluffy. Beat in egg. Add flour mixture in two batches, alternating with banana mixtures. Stir in pecans. Pour into pan, bake until golden brown, brown it about 45 minutes. Let it cool 10 minutes. Run a knife around edge, invert onto a wire rack. Reinsert, let cool. Dust with confectioners sugar, and serve with whipped cream or caramel frosting.

Brownie Puddle Pie

- 1 cup of chopped pecans or pecan pieces
- 14 tbsps of unsalted butter at room temp.
- 1 (3) oz. bar of bittersweet chocolate
- 1/2 cup plus 2 tsps of unsweetened cocoa
- 1 cup plus 3 TBSP of sugar
- 3 large eggs.
- 2 tsp of pure vanilla extract
- 1 (3) oz. pkgs of cream cheese
- 1/2 c. of all purpose four
- 1/2 tsp. of salt
- 2/3 3 OZ. bar if bittersweet chocolate coarsely chopped
- 1/3 cup of liquid heavy cream
- a pinch of salt

Pre heat oven to 325 degrees. Grease removable bottom of a 9 ½ inch pie pan and line with parchment paper. Spray parchment paper with Bakers Joy. Place prepared pan on a cookie sheet to catch any leaks. For the pie, toast pecans on cookie sheet @ 200 degrees for about 5 to 10 minutes, or until lightly browned. Cool completely. In a microwave, melt butter and chocolate. Beat in a large bowl, cocoa, and sugar. Next, beat in eggs and stir in vanilla. Then, beat in cream cheese. Add flour and salt. Mix only until most - don't over mix. Stir in pecans and spread batter into pan. Bake for about 25 to 30 minutes. Cool

Next bake the puddle. In microwave, melt chocolate. Add cream and stir until mixture is smooth. Add a pinch of salt. While pie is still hot and in the cooling stage, insert the bottom of a round spoon or knife and pour the chocolate into little indentations that you have made in the pie with the spoon or knife. Cool and serve. Remove the pan from the brownie when it is cool to the touch. Serve with ice cream or whipped cream.

Browned Butter Cake with Frosting

3/4 c. sugar

2 c. all purpose flour

3/4 c. butter softened

4 egg yolks

2 tsp. vanilla

2 tsp. baking powder

1/8 tsp. salt

3/4 c. half and half

Frosting:

1/4 c. land'o lakes butter

3 c. powdered white confection sugar

3 to 4 TBSP milk

2 tsp. vanilla

Heat oven to 350°. In a large mixer bowl combine sugar and ¾ cup of butter. Beat at medium speed, scraping bowl often, until creamy (1 to 2 minutes). Add egg yolks and vanilla. Continue beating, scraping bowl often until well mixed (1 minute). Reduce speed to low. Beat, gradually adding flour, baking powder and salt alternatively with half and half and scraping bowl often, until well mixed (1 to 2 minute) (batter will be thick). Divide batter between 2 greased and floured 8-inch round cake pans. cool completely. Meanwhile, in 1 quart saucepan melt butter over medium low heat until lightly browned(4 to 5 minutes). In small mixer bowl combine all frosting ingredients except milk. Beat at medium speed, scraping bowl often and gradually adding enough milk for desired spreading consistency. Spread frosting between cooled cake layers, frost entire cake.

Buttermilk Pie

3 eggs

3 TBSP flour

1 c. buttermilk

1/4 tsp. salt

1 1/2 c. sugar

1/2 c. chopped pecans

1/2 c. butter

1 uncooked pie shell

Cream butter, sugar, add eggs one at a time. Combine flour and salt, add small amounts, one at a time. Add buttermilk and pecans. Batter should look like a cake mix that needs more flour. Pour into uncooked pie shell and bake at 300 degrees for 1 ½ hour or until pie is golden brown.

Note: Kitchen Tip: Folding the top crust over the lower crust before crimping will keep the juices in the pie.

Chocolate Ganache Icing

(9-oz.) bitter sweet chopped chocolate

1/2 tsp. salt

1/2 pint heavy whipping cream

Melt chocolate in a bowl. In a saucepan, heat cream to scalding {not boiling}. Pour hot cream over chocolate and stir in salt until mixture is a smooth shiny glaze. Cool before frosting.

Chocolate Leaves

(3-oz.) bittersweet melted chocolate

washed lemon leaves

Only melt chocolate in double boiler. Cool melted chocolate. Use a brush to evenly coat the leaves on its {dull side} backside. Allow to harden in refrigerator. Carefully peel off. Decorate.

Chocolatey Southern Pecan Pie

4 oz. of Sweet Chocolate

3 TBSPS of butter

1 Tsp of brewed or Instant coffee

1/3 cup of sugar

1 cup of light corn syrup

3 eggs slightly beaten

1/2 tsp of salt

1 tsp of pure vanilla extract

1 cup of coarsely chopped pecans

1 unbaked 9 inch pie shell

1 bowl of prepared fresh vanilla heavy whipped cream or whipped topping

Preheat oven to 375 degrees. Heat butter and chocolate over low heat or for 1 minute in the microwave and stir mixture until it has melted and combined to a smooth consistency. Stir in the coffee. Next, bring to a boil over high heat, sugar and syrup, stirring until sugar has dissolved. Reduce the heat and boil on low for about 1 - 2 minutes. Remove from heat. Add the chocolate mixture. Pour ½ cup of chocolate mixute into beaten eggs in order to temper the eggs, without scrambling the eggs. Once combined, put the remaining chocolate mixture over the eggs and stir. Stir in the salt, vanilla and nuts. Pour mixture into pie shell. Bake for 40 to 50 minutes until filling is puffy. Serve with cream topping.

Coffee Ice Cream Pie

(7-oz.) chocolate wafers crumbled

3 1 qt. containers of coffee ice cream

1 TBSP brewed coffee

chocolate sauce

whipped cream

nuts

2 TBSP sugar

2 TBSP melted butter

1/4 tsp. salt

To make crust in mixing bowl, combine wafers, coffee sugar, salt, coffee, and butter until firm. Pack firmly in a pie dish, soften ice cream. Spread over wafer mixture.

Freeze for 1 hour, upon serving, melt 1/3 cup of semi sweet morsels until liquid swirl over whip cream on pie.

Deborah Odom

Cousin Amy's Cream Cheese Pound Cake

4 sticks butter (room temp.)

2 1/3 c. plain flour + 2/3 c. self-rising flour

(8-oz.) cream cheese (room temp.)

2 tsp. vanilla flavoring

6 eggs (room temp.)

2 tsp. butter flavoring

3 c. sugar

Use a hand mixer to cream butter and cream cheese together. Add eggs one at a time. Add flour and mix well. Add flavorings. Bake 1 hour at 250 degrees and then 45 minutes at 300 degrees, {or until done}.This cake is done when it shrinks slightly from the sides of the pan or if it springs back when touched lightly with the finger.

Note: Vacations were usually spent in Gods country; courteously polite people, delicious food, lots of family to visit, and scenery that can only be described as the sister to the countryside of England, ALABAMA! We visited one of our cousins, who served warm cake and chilled farm fresh whole milk, and lots of southern hospitality.

Easy Coconut Pie

3 eggs

1 1/2 c. sugar

4 TBSP butter

1 c. milk

1/2 c. coconut

1 tsp. vanilla

Mix. Pour in unbaked pie shell. Bake 45 minutes at 325 degrees.

Note: The lower crust should be placed in the pan so that it covers the surface smoothly, and be sure no air lurks beneath the surface, for it will push the crust out of shape in baking.

Deborah Odom

Fanciful Fruit Pizza

- 1 roll of Pillsbury refrigerator sugar cookies
- 1/2 c. peach halves or canned (drained)
- 1/2 c. fresh strawberry halves (not frozen)
- 1 (8-oz.) soft cream cheese
- 1/2 c. fresh blueberries (not frozen)
- 1/3 c. sugar
- 1/4 c. sweet orange marmalade
- 1/2 tsp. vanilla

Heat oven to 375 degrees F. Line a pizza dish with aluminum foil. Cut cookie dough with sharp knife in 2/8 slices. Slightly over lap on bottom of lined pan. Bake for 10 minutes. Peel off foil. Cool and combine the soft cream cheese with the sugar, vanilla and beat until blended. Spread over crust. Arrange peach halves, strawberry halves and blueberries on top. Heat the orange marmalade with 1 tbs. of water until just till warm and brush over fruit and cheese. Refrigerate overnight before serving.

Goof Poof Caramel Frosting

1 c. of whole milk

2 1/2 c. sugar

1/2 c. butter

1 tsp. vanilla

1/2 tsp. salt

Bring to a boil in a sauce pan, milk 2 cups of sugar and butter. Stir and cook on medium heat until sugar melts. Remove from heat. Put ½ c. sugar in a skillet and brown it and until melted. Add brown sugar to the mixture in the saucepan. Mix well and cook until it reaches soft ball stage (238° on candy thermometer). Stir frequently remove from heat and add water. Place sauce pan in cold water till cooled. Beat with electric mixture to desired consistency. Frost cake.

Goof Proof Frosting

1 cup milk

2 1/2 cups sugar, divided

1/3 cup butter

1 tsp. vanilla

1/2 tsp salt

In a saucepan bring milk to boil; add 2 cups of sugar and butter. Stir and cook on medium heat until sugar melts; set aside. Put ½ cups sugar in a skillet and cook on low heat. Stirring. Until the sugar melts and turns brown. Add browned sugar to the mixture in the saucepan. Mix well and cook until it reaches soft ball stage (238 degrees on the candy thermometer). Stir frequently. Remove from the heat and add vanilla and salt. Place saucepan in a bowl of cold water and allow frosting to cool. Beat to desired consistency. Will frost a sheet cake; double the recipe for 2 or 3 layer cake.

Aunt Maudie's Lemon Meringue Pie

- 1 graham cracker crumb pie crust
- 1 c. sweetened condensed milk
- 1 TBSP grated lemon and or 1/4 tsp lemon extract
- 2 eggs separated
- 1/4 tsp. cream of tarter
- 1/2 c. lemon juice
- 4 TBSP sugar

Heat oven to 325 degrees F. Combine grated lemon and juice. Stir in eagle brand milk. Add egg yolks and stir until well blended. Pour into chilled graham cracker crumb crust. Next beat cream of tarter into egg whites. Beat until almost stiff to hold. Gradually add sugar, beating until stiff but not dry. Pile lightly on pie filling. Bake for 15 minutes.

Deborah Odom

Grandma Stembridges Favorite Coconut Cake

1 cup of softened butter

2 cups of sugar

3 cups of clour

4 eggs

1 cup of whole milk

3 tsps of baking powder

pinch of salt

1 tsp. of vanilla

Icing

3/4 cups of sugar

1/2 cup of Light Karo syrup

2 TSBP of water

3 Egg Whites

1 Tsbp of Vanilla Flavoring

1 TBSP of Coconut Flavoring

1 8 Oz bag or can of grated or shredded coconut

Preheat oven to 300 degrees. Cream butter and sugar; add eggs and beat after each addition. Add vanilla. Sift cake flour, baking powder and salt together. Add flour mixture and milk alternately ending with milk. Pour into (2) 8 or 9 inch greased and waxed lined pans for about 25 minutes. Cool before icing.

Icing

Cook sugar and syrup with water to spin a thread. Beat egg whites until stiff. Add 1 TBSP of hot sugar syrup to temper egg whites. Beat remaining syrup into egg whites. Add flavorings and frost cooled cake. Sprinkle with coconut.

Grandma Stembridges Pecan Pie

1 cup of dark Karo syrup

1/4 tsp of salt

4 TBSPS of butter

1 tsp of vanilla

1/2 cup of sugar

3 eggs

1 cup of chopped pecans

1 unbaked pie shell

1 cup of chopped pecans

Preheat oven to 275 degrees F. Beat eggs, sugar, flour, salt, vanilla and butter. Add syrup and pecans. Pour into a pie shell and bake for 1 hour.

Deborah Odom

Great Grandma Lillie's Brownie Cakes

2/3 cup of solid shortening

2 cups of sugar

4 eggs well beaten

1/2 cup of cocoa

1 1/2 cups of Plain Flour

1/2 tsp of salt

1 tsp of Baking Powder

2 tsps of Vanilla

Preheat oven to 350 degrees F. Thoroughly cream shortening and sugar. Add eggs and blend in cocoa. Mix and sift dry ingredients. Add to mixture. Add nuts and vanilla. Bake in a 10x14x2 greased pan for 25 minutes. When cake has baked and the inserted toothpick comes out clean. Remove cake from the oven. Spread marshmallow cream of marshmallows and return cake to the oven until the marshmallow cream or marshmallows have a slight golden brown gooiness. Remove from oven while and let the cake rest while you make the icing.

Icing

1.2 sticks of butter

2 cups of Confectioner Sugar

1.2 cup of Pet milk

1/4 cup of cocoa

1/4 tsp of salt

Bring to a boil, milk and butter. Remove from burner and add confectioner sugar, salt and cocoa. Spread evenly over cake and garnish with chopped pecans.

Great, Great Grandmas' Tea Cakes

2 c. plain flour

1 tsp. baking soda

1 c. sugar

1 egg

1/2 c. butter or cooking oil

1 tsp. vanilla flavoring

1/4 c. butter milk

Heat oven to 350 degrees. Mix all of the ingredients together, Roll in ¼ of thick cookie dough, and cut with cookie cutter. Bake on a lightly greased cookie sheet. Bake for 9 to 12 minutes.

Note: When mother was little, she frequently visited her grandmother who gave her the job to go out into the massive gardens and pick flowers for arrangements throughout the house. Her reward was baking these mouthwatering cookies with grandma.

Deborah Odom

Holiday Pumpkin Cake

- 1 18 1/4-ounce pkg. yellow cake mix
- 1 tsp. vanilla
- 1 egg 8 TBSP butter, melted
- 8 TBSP butter, melted
- 1 (16-oz.) box powdered sugar

- 1 (8-oz.) pkg. cream cheese, softened
- 1 tsp. cinnamon
- 1 (15-oz.) can pumpkin
- 1 tsp. all spice
- 3 eggs
- 1/2 tsp. salt

To make the cake combine all of the ingredients and mix well with an electric mixer. Pat the mixture into the bottom of a lightly greased 13 by 9 inch baking pan. Bake at the 350 degrees to make the filling. In a large bowl, beat the cream cheese and the pumpkin until smooth. Add the eggs, vanilla, and butter, and beat together. Next, add the powdered sugar, cinnamon all spice, salt, and mix well. Spread pumpkin mixture over cake batter and bake for 40 to 50 min. Make sure not to over bake as the center should be a little gooey. Serve with fresh whipped cream.

Lime Pie Frozen Delight Treat

1 can of condensed milk

1 graham cracker pie shell

can crushed pineapple in heavy syrup

crushed pecans

1 lime aid frozen (thaw)

1 thinly sliced lime slices

2 qt. thawed cool whip

Mix 1 qt of Cool Whip with all of the other ingredients together. Spread into pie shell. Sprinkle pecans on top. Refrigerate. Reserve one qt of Cool Whip. Serve with a dollop of cool whip, and a lime slice.

Note: A July the 4th favorite. Always keep these ingredients on hand for an easy desert.

Deborah Odom

Mississippi Mud Cake

Cake:

2 c. sugar

1 jar marshmallow cream

1 1/3 c. flour {plain}

2 sticks butter

4 eggs

3 tsp. vanilla

3 melted squares of unsweetened chocolate

Frosting:

1/3 c. cocoa frosting

1/3 c. canned milk

1 tsp. vanilla

2 sticks butter

1 box white confection sugar

1/4 tsp. salt

1 c. chopped pecans

Heat oven to 350 degrees F. Cream sugar, butter and sift flour, cocoa, and salt. Add to cream mixture. Mix well. Add vanilla and nuts. Pour into greased and floured pan.

Bake for 35 minutes. Remove from oven and pour the marshmallow cream on it. Bake for another 5 to 10 minutes until it turns a buttery color.

Frosting Directions:

Beat well mixing sugar, melted butter, melted chocolate squares and vanilla Add milk. Spread on cake. Sprinkle nuts on top.

Note: A family reunion favorite.

Mothers Old Time Southern Fruitcake

- 1 lb. of butter at room temp.
- 4 TBSP of bourbon extract flavoring
- 1 pkg, of seedless raisins
- 2 1/4 c. of sugar
- 2 containers of sliced red and green candied pineapple (Reserve some whole slices to decorate the top of the cake)
- 2 containers of sliced white candied pineapple (Reserve some whole slices to decorate the top of the cake)
- 12 eggs at room temp.
- 1 1/2 c. of blanched almonds
- 1 1/2 c. of juice of an orange
- 1 pkg. of gold seedless raisins
- 2 oz. of candied orange and lemon peel
- 1 16 oz container of mixed candied fruit
- 1 container of candied red cherries (Reserve some to decorate the top of the cake)
- 1 container of candied green cherries (Reserve some to decorate the top of the cake
- 4 c. of all purpose flour
- 1 c. of shredded coconut (Toasted is optional)
- 2 1/2 tsp. of baking powder
- 1 tsp. of salt
- 1/2 lb. of pitted dates cut in half
- 1/2 lb of dried figs
- 4 1/2 c of chopped pecans
- 1/2 tsp of ground nutmeg
- 1 TBSP of dark molasses

Preheat oven to 350 degrees. Cream butter. Add 1 cup and 2 tbsp of sugar. Beat in till light. Sift flour, salt, baking powder and nutmeg together. Beat egg yolks until thick. Add to the rest of the mixture. Add molasses, fruit and stir well. Remember to reserve some of the candied fruit to decorate the top of the cake. Bake until tops of cake are lightly brown. Cook in a greased tube pan or little individual loaf pans. Will keep in the refrigerator for 4-6 weeks and the freezer for 3-4 months.

Deborah Odom

Mothers Peach Cobbler

1/2 cup unsalted butter, melted

1/8 tsp salt

1 cup all purpose flour

1 cup milk

1 cup sugar

1 large can of peaches in its own juice

3 tsp baking powder

Preheat oven to 375 degrees. Pour the melted butter into a 13 by 9 by 2-inch baking dish. In a medium bowl, combine the flour, 1 cup sugar, the baking powder, and the salt and mix well. Stir in the milk, mixing until just combined. Pour this batter over the butter but do not stir them together. Pour the peaches over the batter but do not stir them together. Bake in the preheated oven for 40 to 45 minutes or until the top is golden-brown.

My Prize-Winning Chocolate Sheet Cake

2 cups Sifted cake flour	1 cup Water
1/8 tsp. Salt	6 TBSP Cocoa
2 cups Sugar	6 TBSP Milk
2 tsps. Vanilla	1/2 cup Buttermilk
2 sticks Butter	1 tsp. baking soda
1 box confectioner's sugar	1 cup pecans chopped
1/2 cup Vegetable Oil	2 Eggs, beaten

Cooking utensil: large greased and floured sheet cake pan
Preheat oven: 350 degrees

Cooking time: 20 minutes. Mix flour and sugar together. Combine 1 stick of butter, oil, water and 3 TBSP cocoa in sauce pan and bring to boil. Pour flour and 2 cups sugar. Mix well. Dissolve baking soda in buttermilk. To the chocolate mix, add beaten eggs, salt, vanilla and buttermilk-baking soda. Mix, beating after each addition. Bake in sheet cake pan. Then ice. Combine 1 stick of butter, 3 TBSP cocoa and 6 TBSP milk in saucepan and bring to a boil. Add confectioner's sugar and vanilla. Mix well. Add chopped pecans. Spread on top of cake while warm.

Deborah Odom

Cousin Linda's Oatmeal Meltaways

1 1/2 c. oatmeal

1 c. sugar

1/8 tsp. salt

1/2 lb. butter

1 1/4 c. flour

Cream margarine and sugar. Add oatmeal, flour, and salt mixture gradually. Chill for 1 hour. Roll into small balls and press down with a fork. Bake at 350 degrees for 15 minutes. Cool. Sprinkle with powdered sugar.

Over the Top Pecan Squares

Crust :

1 1/4 pound unsalted butter, room temperature

3/4 cup granulated sugar

3 extra-large eggs

3/4 tsp. pure vanilla extract

4 1/2 cups all-purpose flour

1/2 tsp. baking powder

1/4 tsp. salt

Topping:

1 pound unsalted butter

1 cup good honey

1/2 cup of molasses

3 cups light brown sugar, packed

1/4 cup heavy cream

2 pound pecans, coarsely chopped

1 tsp. vanilla

Preheat the oven to 350 degree. Crust instructions: beat the butter and granulated sugar in the bowl of an electric mixer, until light, for about 3 minutes. Add the eggs and the vanilla and mix well. Sift together the flour, baking powder, and salt. Mix the dry ingredients into the batter with the mixer on low speed until just combined. Press the dough evenly into an ungreased 18 by 12 by 1-inch baking sheet, making an edge around the outside. It will be very sticky; sprinkle the dough and your hands lightly with flour. Bake for 15 minutes, until the crust is set but not browned. Cool.

Topping instructions: Combine the butter, honey, molasses, brown sugar, and vanilla in a large, heavy-bottomed saucepan.

Cook over low heat until the butter is melted, using a wooden spoon to stir. raise the heat and boil for 3 minutes. Remove from the heat. Stir in the heavy cream and pecans. Pour over the crust, trying not to get the filling between the crust and the pan. Bake for 25 to 30 minutes, until the filling is set.

Remove from the oven and allow to cool. After it has chilled put it in the refrigerator.

Pecan Tastiest

Crust:	2 c. broken pecans
(3-oz.) cream cheese	3 tsp. vanilla
3 sticks butter	3 eggs
3 c. sifted flour	3 pinch dashes of salt
Filling:	1 box light brown sugar
3 TBSP butter	

Heat oven to 325 degrees. Let cream cheese and 3 sticks of butter soften at room temperature. Stir in flour and chill 1 hour. Shape into 6 dozen, 1 inch balls ;place in very small ungreased muffin tins. Press dough against bottom and sides. Fill with the following. Filling Directions : beat eggs;add sugar, 3 tbs of butter vanilla, and salt. Mix enough to be smooth. Add pecans. Bake in slow oven for 25 minutes. Cool BEFORE REMOVING.

Peach Pie Delight

2 c. of flour

3 c. confectioners sugar

1 c. softened butter

2 c. pie peach fillings

1 c. crushed pecans

2 envelopes dream whip

8 oz. cream cheese

1 c. nuts

Heat oven to 350 degrees F. Make the crust using flour, butter and crushed pecans. Press into a pie pan and bake for 20 minutes. Allow to cool completely before putting in the filling. Filling: Mix cream cheese and sugar together. Next, in s separate bowl, prepare the dream whip as directed on the package. Fold in cream cheese and sugar mixture, into dream whip. Fold in peaches pie filling and nuts. Spread onto crust.

Chill overnight.

Pineapple Cream Pie

1 (9-oz.) cool whip or 1 box of Dream Whip prepared as directed on pkg.

1/4 c. pineapple juice

1/2 c. pecans

1 can sweet condensed milk

4 tsp. lemon juice (Start with 1 tsp. and vary according to taste)

1 (16-oz.) can drained pineapple

Mix well together and pour into graham cracker crust. Chill before servings

Pineapple Delight Bundt Cake

1 pkg. yellow cake mix {butter or pudding }

1/4 c. coconuts

1/2 (8-oz.) c. crushed drained pineapple in heavy syrup

4 eggs

1 c. chopped pecans

1 3 1/8 oz instant vanilla pudding

1/2 c. vegetable oil

1 c. pineapple juice

1/4 c. syrup from pineapple can

Glaze Syrup:

1/2 c. butter

1 c. sugar

1/4 c. sater

Sprinkle ½ c nuts on bottom of greased tube pan. Mix all ingredients. Pour mixture over nuts. Bake 1 hour at 325 degrees. For glaze syrup combine ingredients and boil 3 minutes. Pour slowly over cooked cake until all ingredients are absorbed.

Deborah Odom

Pineapple Treat

- 1 {18-25 - oz } box yellow cake mix, plus ingredients to prepare
- 1 box French vanilla pudding, plus ingredients to prepare
- 1 tsp. butter flavor to cake mix
- 1 1/2 c. heavy cream
- 1 (20-oz.) can crushed pineapple
- 1 c. flaked, sweetened toasted coconut
- 1/3 c. sugar
- 1/2 tsp. salt

Prepare yellow cake mix as directed using a greased 13 by 9 by 2 - inch pan and bake at 350 degrees for 30 to 35 minutes. While cake is baking, combine the pineapple, salt, and 1/3 cup of sugar in saucepan, and bring to a boil over medium heat stirring constantly. Remove from heat and allow to cool slightly. Remove cake from oven and using a fork, pierce holes into cake. Pour pineapple mixture over hot cake and set aside. Prepare pudding according to package directions. Spread pudding over cake and refrigerate until through chilled. Whip heavy cream and remaining sugar until stiff.

Cover top cake with whipped cream and sprinkle toasted coconut on top.

Royal Icing

1-lb. Confectioner's sugar   5 tsp. Meringue powder

1/3 c. Water   1 tsp. Vanilla

Beat with electric mixer at slow speed until mixture turns white.

Deborah Odom

Strawberry Cake

- 1 pkg. drain frozen strawberries
- 3 eggs whipped 5 minutes
- 1 box blend white cake mix
- 1 small pkg of dry strawberry jello
- 1 box confection sugar
- 1/8 tsp. salt
- 1/2 c. water
- 4 TBSP melted butter
- 1/2 c. oil
- 1 qt. strawberry juice

Preheat oven to 350 degrees f. Drain the 1 pkg of frozen strawberries. Whip the 3 eggs for 5 minutes. Add the oil and the water. Blend the cake mix with the dry strawberry jello into the eggs, oil and water mixture. Fold in the strawberries. Grease with oil (2) round 9 x 9 inch pans. Bake in the center of oven for 25-30 minutes.

Frosting: Mix the confectioner sugar, salt, melted butter and the strawberry juice.

Spread generously on each layer and swirl the top.

Note: Kitchen Tip :Try using a thread instead of a knife when a cake is to be cut while it is hot.

Miss Willadene's Fav's

Strawberry Parfait

1 can of chilled carnation milk

1 box of vanilla wafers

1 pkg. of strawberries

1 TBSP lemon juice

4 TBSP sugar

Mint leaves or charred mint chocolate

Whip milk. Mix lemon juice, sugar, and strawberries. Line the bottom and sides of a large glass dish with vanilla wafers. Pour mixture (milk, lemon juice, sugar, and strawberries in dish.) Top with mint leaves or charred mint chocolate. Refrigerate overnight.

Note: Great for a summer day.

Deborah Odom

Sweet Nothings - Rugelach

- 2 sticks Unsalted Softened Butter
- 1 cup Good quality Apricot Jelly (Not Jam)
- 2 TBSP Granulated Sugar
- 1 (8-oz.) carton Dairy Sour Cream
- 1/2 cup Finely Chopped Pecans
- 1 large Egg Yolk
- 1 1/2 tsp. Ground Cinnamon
- 2 cups All Purpose Flour
- 1/4 cup Unsalted Softened Butter
- 1/4 tsp. Salt
- 1/2 cup Granulated Sugar
- 1/2 cup Finely chopped golden raisins
- 2-3 tsp. Powdered Sugar

Preheat oven to 350 degrees. In a large bowl, with an electric mixer on low, beat 2 sticks of butter for 30 seconds. Beat in 2 tablespoons of granulated sugar; until light and fluffy. Next, beat in sour cream and egg yolk. With a wooden spoon, stir in flour and salt just until all ingredients are mixed. In a glass bowl, cover and chill for 1 hour or until dough is easy to handle. For the filling, combine nuts, raisins, ½ cup granulated sugar, ¼ cup butter, and apricot jelly. Dust with flour a marble slab or wooden board. With a wooden or marble rolling pin, roll a ¼ dough into a 10 -inch circle. Then spread ¼ of the filling over the circle. Cut dough into 12 wedges. Just like you would a crescent, roll up each wedge, starting at wide end. Repeat. Place 2 inches apart on foil-lined or parchment paper metal cookie sheet, Bake for 25 minutes. Cool on sheet 1 minute. Transfer to wire rack to cool. Sprinkle powdered sugar or a mixture of cinnamon and powdered sugar, or one of my favorites, drizzle with semi sweet melted chocolate.

Note: Sundays mornings were always very busy at our house. Whether it was hurrying to Sunday School, attending Choir Practice or picking up guests for church, these on-the-go delicacies have been a favorite for a quick Sunday morning snack. They won't bloat you up like a bagel and they are not icky sweet like a doughnut.

Deborah Odom

The Best $150 Chocolate Coconut Cake

- 1 cup creamery unsalted butter for the cake batter & 4 tbs. for the frost
- 1/2 cup buttermilk mixed with 1 tablespoon vinegar
- 4 eggs
- 1 tsp. vanilla for the cake batter & 1 tsp for the frosting
- 2 cup sugar
- 2 cup cake flour (sifted)
- 1 can flaked cocoanut
- 1 tsp. soda
- 3/4 cup All purpose flour
- 1/2 tsp. salt for the cake & an additional 1/4 tsp for the frosting
- 2 cups whole milk
- 8 squares Hershey's chocolate (melt with butter in top of double boiler)

Preheat oven: 350. METHOD: in an electric mixer pour sugar, chocolate-butter mixture - whip 1 minute. Add all whole eggs - whip 1 minute. Add vanilla and ½ cup buttermilk. Sift dry ingredients. Add alternately with remainder of liquid. Whip 3 minutes. Fold in 2/3 coconut. Grease 2 round 9 x 9 pans with oil. Pour in batter. Set in center of oven. Bake 30 to 35 minutes. Cool on racks. Frosting & Filling (for best results use Hershey's chocolate). In the same double boiler (do not wash) melt 4 squares chocolate, 4 tablespoons creamery butter. Add 2 cups of milk - heat until very hot. In another bowl, lend 1 cup sugar and ¾ cup all - purpose flour thoroughly with ¼ teaspoon salt. Dump all at once into hot liquid - stir vigorously until very thick. Add 1 teaspoon vanilla and 1/3 can cocoanut. Frost and fill the layers and outside of cake.

Note: Fill cake pans about two-thirds full and spread batter well into corners and to the sides, leaving a slight hollow in the center.

The Best Easy Fudge Frosting

4 squares bakers unsweetened chocolate

2 TBSP butter

1 tsp. vanilla

4 c. powdered sugar

1 tsp. salt

1/2 c. of Heavy Cream

Melt chocolate and butter. Beat in remaining ingredients until well blended and smooth. Spread quickly. If frosting becomes too thick add milk by teaspoons.

Deborah Odom

Aunt Mallie's Toffee Squares

- 3 large eggs
- 1/4 tsp. salt
- 1 oz. box yellow cake mix
- 1 1/2 TBSP pure vanilla extract
- 1 box of white confectioners sugar
- 1 stick unsalted butter, melted
- 1 (8-oz.) package cream cheese, softened
- 1 cup Hershey's toffee nugget candy
- 1 stick unsalted butter, melted

Preheat the oven to 350 degrees. Lightly butter a 13 by-2-inch baking pan. With an electric mixer, combine the cake mix, 1 egg, 1 stick of butter and ½ tsp. vanilla. Mix well. Press into the bottom of prepared pan and wait for filling. Next using an electric mixer, beat the cream cheese until smooth. Beat in the 2 eggs, 1 TBSP vanilla, & salt. Add confectioners' sugar and beat well. Reduce the speed and slowly pour in butter. Mix well. Fold in toffee bits. Pour filling onto cake mixture. Bake for 35 to 45 minutes. Remember that the middle is supposed to be gooey but not raw! Let cool. Serve with coffee ice-cream.

Miss Willadene's Fav's

COOKIES & CANDY

TIPS FOR COOKIES AND CANDY

❈ Cookie sheets should clear the oven by about w inches.

❈ Cool cookies completely before storing them into airtight containers.

❈ Limp cookies can be revived by placing them in a 300 degree oven for 3 minutes.

❈ Baked cookies can be frozen up to 4 months.

❈ Mailing cookies? Use drop or bar cookies.

❈ A wire cheese slicer will cut a roll of chilled cookie dough with ease.

❈ CANDY TEMPERATURES:

232 to 234 F.	Frostings, syrups. Syrup forms a soft thread.
234 to 240 F.	Fudge, fondant. Syrup forms a soft ball.
242 to 248 F.	Caramels. Firm ball forms.
250 to 268 F.	Taffy, divinity. Hardball.
270 to 288 F.	Toffee. Soft crack.
209 10 310 F.	Hard candies. Hard brittle crack.

Deborah Odom

A Recipe for Preserving Children

1 large grassy field	3 small dogs
1 hot sun	Deep blue sky
6 children	1 narrow pebbly brook
Flowers	lots and lots of giggles

Place children and dogs into the field. Mix and stir continuously. Sprinkle the field with flowers. Pour the brook gently over the pebbles. Cover all with a deep blue sky and bake in the hot sun. When children have rosy cheeks, remove them and place them into a cool bath.

Aunt Maudie's Alabama Peanut Brittle

3 cups sugar

1 qt. peanut (raw)

1 cups white corn syrup

1/2 inch paraffin

1/2 cup water

3 tsp's of baking soda

In a heavy pot, cook sugar, corn syrup, water, and paraffin until it forms a hard ball in cold water. Use a candy thermometer just to be sure it reaches the hardball stage. Add peanuts and cook until they are brown. Remove from heat, add soda and stir until crunchy. Pour out on a buttered round cake pan. Let cool and break into small pieces.

Note: During the fall, mother liked to take us to the Worlds Largest Peanut Fair in Dothan Alabama. Sometimes, school dates interfered. So, mother would send for some Alabama peanuts. We would have a nutty afternoon, making crunchy tasty peanut brittle. We even boiled peanuts and served them in pint size brown paper bags - just like they used at the fair.

Deborah Odom

Buttery Pecan Turtles

Crust:

2 c. purpose flour

1 c. firmly pakd. brown sugar

1/2 c. butter, softened

1 c. whole pecan pieces

Filling:

2/3 c. butter

1/2 c. firmly packed brown sugar

1 c. milk chocolate chips

1/4 tsp. salt

Heat oven to 350 degrees. In large mixer bowl combine all crust ingredients except pecans. Beat at medium speed, scraping bowl often, until well mixed and particles are fine (2 to 3 minutes). Press on bottom of 13x9 inch baking pan. Sprinkle pecans evenly onver unbaked crust. In 1 qt. sauce pan combine butter and brown sugar. Cook over medium heat, stirring constantly. Add salt. Pour evenly over pecans and crust. Bake 18 to 22 minutes or until entire caramel layer is bubbly. Remove from oven. Immediately sprinkle with chips; allow melt slightly (2 to 3 minutes). Swirl chips leaving some whole for a marbled effect. Cool completely; cut into bars.

Miss Willadene's Fav's

Chocolate & Peanut Butter Truffles

Ingredients:

3/4 c. Butter

1 c. Reese's peanut butter chips

1 (14-oz.) can Eagle brand sweetened condensed milk (not evaporated milk)

1/2 c. Hershey's cocoa

1 TBSP of Vanilla extract

TOPPINGS/ COATINGS:

#1 1/2 c. of unsweetened cocoa

2: finely chopped (crushed) peanuts or pecans

3: 1/2 cup of graham cracker crumbs

In heavy saucepan, over low heat, melt chips with butter. Stir in cocoa until smooth. Add sweetened condensed milk and vanilla, cook and stir until thickened and well blended about 4 min. Remove from heat. Chill 2 hours or until firm enough to handle. Shape into 1-inch balls. Roll in any of the above coatings. Chill until firm, about 1 hour. Store covered in refrigerator.

Deborah Odom

Cookie Kiss

1 c. butter or margarine, softened

1 c. finely chopped pecans

1/2 c. sugar

36 Hershey kisses

1 T. vanilla

1 box confectioners sugar

1 3/4 c. all purpose flour

Heat oven to 375 degrees F. Cream butter, sugar and vanilla in large mixed bowl. Gradually add salt flower and nuts ;beat on low speed until well blended. Chill dough about 1 hour or until firm enough to handle. Mold about 1 tablespoon of dough around an unwrapped chocolate kiss and roll to a ball. Be sure to cover kiss completely. Place on an ungreased cookie sheet. Bake 12 minutes or until cookies set, but not brown. Cool slightly; remove to wire rack. While still warm, roll in confections sugar. cool. store in tightly cover container. Roll in sugar again before serving, if desired.

Note: MEASURE!!! Dip the spoon in hot water to measure lard, butter, etc. The fat will slip out more easily.

Crispy Ginger Snaps

3 cups all-purpose flour

1/2 cup (1 stick) unsalted butter, softened

1 1/2 tsp. baking soda

1 cup sugar

1 1/2 tsp. cinnamon

1/2 cup dark corn syrup

1 1/2 tsp. ground ginger

1/2 tsp. salt

1 1/2 tsp. ground cloves

Garnish:

1/4 cup Sliced almonds

1 TBSP of cooled instant coffee

1 c. of confectioner sugar

Heat oven to 400 degrees F. In a bowl, sift together flour, baking soda, spices plus salt. In a medium bowl with an electric mixer beat cream until it just holds stiff speaks. In another large bowl beat butter and sugar until mixture is light and fluffy. On low speed, beat in corn syrup and whipped cream, beating until cream is just combined. Add flour mixture and beat until combined. Form dough into a disk, wrap in plastic and chill until firm, for at least 2 hours, and up to 2 days. When ready to use, cut the dough into quarters. Cover the remaining quarters with plastic and put them into the refrigerator. Work with 1 quarter at a time. Flour a marble slab or wooden board and rolling pin so that you can roll out dough into a round circle. Roll the dough as thin as possible. Use cutters dipped in flour to cut out cookies. Place cookies onto cut to an ungreased baking sheets. about ½-inch apart, and top each with an almond slice. Use up all the dough. Bake cookies in batches in upper and lower thirds of oven, switching position of sheets halfway through baking, until cookies puff and then collapse slightly, about 6 minutes. Cool cookies on aluminum foil. Stir confectioner sugar with coffee and drizzle over cookies.

Note: World War II, the Korean War and Pearl Harbor were tough years. My mother and grandmother would bake cookies to send to the military service men and women. With 6 of her own brothers fighting in the wars at one time, they felt that it was good to try to send a little love from home to so many who were protecting our great country.

Double Chocolate Treasures

- 1 (12-oz.) pkg. (2 cups) semi-sweet chocolate pieces
- 2 c. Quaker oats (quick 1 min oats uncooked)
- 1/2 c. margarine
- 1 1/2 c. all purpose flour
- 3/4 c. sugar
- 2 tsp. baking powder
- 2 eggs
- 1/4 tsp. salt
- 1 tsp. vanilla
- 1/2 c. powdered sugar

Heat oven to 350 degrees F. In heavy saucepan over low heat, melt 1 cup chocolate pieces. Stir until smooth, cool slightly. Beat together margarine and sugar until light and fluffy. Blend eggs, vanilla and melted chocolate. Add combined dry ingredients except powdered sugar, stir in remaining chocolate pieces. Shape dough into 1 inch balls, roll in powdered sugar, coating heavily. Place on ungreased cookies sheets, bake 10 to 12 minutes. Cool for 1 minute on cookie sheet, remove to wire rack. Store in airtight container. Makes about 5 dozen. *NOTE* to microwave, place chocolate pieces in glass container. Microwave at HIGH to 1 ½ min. Stir after 1 min. Stir until chocolate is melted and smooth.

Note: You may determine the age of an egg by placing it in the bottom of a bowl of cold water. If it lays on its side, it is strictly fresh. If it stands at an angle it is at least three days old and ten days old if it stands on end.

Easy Lollipops

1 cup Sugar

1 cup tap water

2/3 cup light corn syrup

food coloring

Mix sugar, water and syrup over medium heat, stirring constantly until mixture reaches 300 degrees on a candy thermometer. Remove from heat. Add desired color. Pour onto aluminum foil in desired sizes and place stick into lollipop. Allow to cool.

Makes 12 pops.

Note: Flavor Option: Go into a professional kitchen supply store or online and purchase different flavorings such as grape, cherry, watermelon etc, and stir into the sugar, water and syrup mixture.

Florentine Cookies

2/3 c. butter

2 c. uncooked quick oats

1 c. brown sugar

1/4 c. white sugar

2/3 c. all purpose flavor

1/4 c. corn syrup light

1/4 c. milk

1/4 tsp. salt

1 tsp. vanilla

1 pkg. semi sweet chocolate morsels (2 cups) 375. F for 5-7 min

Preheat oven to 375 degrees. Melt butter in microwave. Stir butter into oats, sugar, flavor, corn syrup, milk, vanilla, extranet, and salt mix well. Drop teaspoon full, onto foil lined or splat cookies sheet spread thin rounds. Bake 5-7 minutes and cool. Filling: Semi sweet chocolate melted in microwave. Dip ½ cookie in chocolate. Cool on foil or wax paper.

Deborah Odom

Heavenly Chocolate Drops

1 (12-oz.) package chocolate chips

1 cup flour

1 can eagle condensed milk

1 tsp. salt

1/2 stick butter or margarine

1 tsp. vanilla

1 cup nuts (if desired)

Preheat oven to 350 degrees. Mix chips, milk, and butter in microwave or double broiler. Cool. Next, stir in flour, salt, vanilla and nuts.

Mix together and drop by teaspoon onto foil covered oven rack (Works better then cookie sheets). Bake 7 minutes. Do not overcook. Cookies must be eaten the same day.

Note: As a kid coming home from school, nothing smelled better to my brother and I, then when we walked into our home and mother had a plate of homemade cookies for us to munch on. The perfect condiment? A tall glass of chilled whole milk.

Irresistible Chocolate Chip Cookies

- 3/4 cup Crisco Shortening Solid
- 1 3/4 cup all-purpose flour
- 1 1/4 tsp. firmly pkg. light brown sugar
- 1 1/4 tsp. salt
- 2 TBSP milk
- 3/4 TBSP baking soda
- 1 TBSP pure vanilla extract
- 1 1/2 cup semi-sheet chocolate chips
- 1 large or extra large egg
- 1 cup chopped pecans

Pre heat oven to 375 degrees. Place sheets of foil on countertop for cooling cookies. Combine Crisco, brown sugar, milk, and vanilla in large bow. Beat at medium speed with electric mixer until well blended. Beat egg into creamed mixture. Combine flour, salt, and baking soda. Mix into creamed mixture just until blended. Stir in chocolate chips and nuts. Drop by rounded teaspoons onto an ungreased cookie sheet. Bake at 375 degrees for 8-10 minutes for chewy cookies and 11 - 13 minutes for crisp cookies.

Deborah Odom

Pecan Crunch

6 c. plain flour

3 TBSP water

3 sticks of butter

3 c. broken pecans

3 sticks oleo

1 box confectioner sugar

6 TBSP heaping sugar

Heat oven to 300 degrees F. Let butter and oleo soften at room temperature. Stir in flour, sugar, water, vanilla and pecans. Roll into one inch balls. Bake in slow oven for about 30-35 minutes or until light brown. When cool, roll in confectioner sugar.

Cousin April's Reindeer Crunch

2 c. rice Krispies

2 c. peanuts

2 c. captain crunch

1 bar white almond bar

2 c. mini marshmallows

Mix all ingredients. Put ingredients in a microwave dish and microwave for 90 seconds. If not completely melted, use 15 second intervals until melted. Pull apart and drop into shape on wax paper until stiff. The form should be abstract and about the size of the palm of your hand.

Snowballs

1 (12-oz.) pkg. Dates (chop fine)

4 butter cookies crumbles

(8-oz.) Pecans, Chopped

1 large bag coconut

1 large can crushed pineapple including juice

6 envelopes dream whip or prepared Dream Whip Mix

4 boxes Butter cookies

2 c. miniature marshmallows

Mix together dates, pecans, pineapple, marshmallows, and 4 butter cookies crumbled. Let stand overnight. Spread between 4 butter cookies. Frost all over with dream whip. Cover with cocoanut. Chill until served.

Delicious. These will keep for a week.

Sweet Pecan Sandies

1 c. pecans

2/3 c. confectioner sugar

2 c. all purpose flour

2 tsp. vanilla extract

1 c. softened unsalted butter (2 sticks)

1 tsp. salt

1 c. white granulated sugar

1/2 tsp. bkg. Powder

*Pre heat oven 350 F. Spread the nuts on a layer sheet pan and bake them at 350 degrees for about 10-15 minutes. Cool. With electric beater, beat granulated sugar and butter until creamy. Add the vanilla, flour, bkg.powder, and salt until combined. Roll dough into logs. Refrigerate dough for at least 3 hours. Cut slices of chilled dough and roll into ¼ inch balls. Bake cookies on ungreased cookie sheets at 325 degrees for 15-20 minutes. While cookies are warm, roll in sifted confectioner sugar.

Traditional Rocky Road Fudge

4 c. sugar

1 (7-oz.) jar marshmallow cream

2 c. mini marshmallows

1 (12-oz.) can evaporated milk

2 tsp. vanilla

1/2 c. butter

2 (12-oz.) pkgs. semi sweet chocolate

2 c. nuts

In a 4 qt. Pan, combine sugar, butter, and evaporated milk. Cook over medium heat, stirring occasionally until mix boils (7 to 10 minutes). Boil constantly until candy thermometer reaches 228 degrees. Remove from heat, gradually stir in chocolate chips until melted, stir in marshmallow cream until blended. Add vanilla and marshmallow and nuts. Cover in refrigerator until cool.

Deborah Odom

Ultimate Chocolate Brownies

3 sticks butter

1 TBSP vanilla extract

6 (1-oz.) squares unsweetened chocolate

1 c. chopped pecans

1 1/2 c. all purpose flour

1 tsp. baking soda

1/2 tsp. salt

4 large eggs

3/4 c. confectioner's sugar, sifted

2 c. sugar

Glaze:

1/4 c. of heavy cream

1 c. of semi sweet chocolate chips

Preheat oven 350 f and grease 13 -x- 9 - inch baking pan. In microwave melt butter and unsweetened chocolate until smooth, stirring frequently {1-2 minutes at high} Cool slightly. Stir salt and baking soda into flour. In larger bowl, with electric mixer at low speed, beat eggs one at a time, sugar, and vanilla until well blended. Gradually add chocolate mixture and then flour mixture, until well blended. Add pecans. Pour batter into prepared pan. Bake 35 minutes, or until toothpick inserted in center comes out clean. Cool in pan on wire rack. Meanwhile, to prepare glaze, stir cream and chocolate together over low heat until chocolate is melted and smooth. Remove from heat stir confectioner's sugar until smooth and thickened. Spread over brownies in pan.

Cool and cut into 3- x- 3 - inch squares.

Miss Willadene's Fav's

THIS & THAT.

A Must - Take Time for Ten Things

1 pound of Work

Several loaves of Friendship

1 gal. of Think

Multiple cupfulls of Love

1 heap of Play

Spoonfulls of Dreams

1 pkg. of Read

Heaping Laughs

1 bunch of Worship

1. Take time to WORK --- it is the price of success.
2. Take time to THINK --- it is the source of power.
3. Take time to PLAY --- it is the secret of youth.
4. Take time to READ --- it is the foundation of knowledge.
5. Take time to WORSHIP --- it is the highway of reverence and washes the dust of earth from our eyes.
6. Take time to help and enjoy FRIENDS --- it is the source of happiness.
7. Take time to LOVE --- it is the one sacrament of life.
8. Take time to DREAM --- it hitches the soul to the stars.
9. Take time to LAUGH --- it is the singing that helps with life's loads.
10. Take time to PLAN --- it is the secret of being able to have time to take time for the first nine things.

Deborah Odom

A Williamsburg Potpourri

- 1 qt. dried roses or flower petals
- 1/2 oz. anise seed
- 1 oz. ground cinnamon
- 2 oz. powdered arrowroot
- 1 oz. ground nutmeg
- a handful crushed whole cloves
- 1 oz. ground cloves
- a handful crushed and whole cinnamon
- 1 oz. sliced gingerroot sticks
- small pine cones

Mix dried petals, ground cinnamon, nutmeg, cloves, gingerroot, anise seed, and arrowroot. Store in covered jar. When company comes, place potpourri in a displayed basket, bowl or glass dish.

Note: Dried fruit such as oranges, apples, and/or herbs such as lavender, or rosemary may be added.

Miss Willadene's Fav's

Almond - Parmesan Cheese Spread

- 3 TBSP chopped nuts
- 3 TBSP butter
- 1/4 tsp. salt
- 1/8 tsp pepper
- 3 TBSP minced flat leaf parsley
- 6 TBSP grated pamesean cheese
- 12 buttered toast strips

Saute butter, almonds, parsley, salt and pepper for 2 minutes. Add cheese. Cut bread into strips. Bake white buttered bread at 425 degrees for 10-11 minutes until crispy. Spread cheese mixture on toast while toast is warm.

Basic White Sauce

- 2 TBSP butter or margarine
- 1/2 tsp. salt
- 2 TBSP flour
- 1 c. milk

Heat all ingredients, stirring for 1 minute. If you want a thicker sauce, add flour and butter by TBSP's untill you reach the desired consistency.

Into this sauce you can add cooked vegetables, a little cheese, and what I like is a little bit of cardemon, it has such a nice taste and you can use it in other recipes, such as in baking. Try and see if the thickness of the sauce is to your liking, if not, add more milk or more flour.

Bubble Solution

1/3 c. dish soap or baby shampoo

1 drop food coloring

1 1/2 c. water

plastic container

2 tsp. sugar

Combine and pour into a container. Use a plastic straw or pipe cleaner to make your own designs to blow.

Bubbles Galore

2 cups warm water

1 TBSP glycerin(optional)

2 TBSP liquid detergent

1 drop of food coloring (optional)

1 TBSP sugar

Combine ingredients. The glycerin will make the bubbles iridescent. Pour into empty containers. If the children are playing outside, place a fly swatter in the soap mixture and swing it around to make lots of big bubbles.

Canning Figs by Cousin Betty Clyde

3 4 lb. bags (or 12 lbs.) of a dozen figs

1 Dutch oven

4 lbs. of sugar

Cook on top of the stove. Open 1 bag of figs at a time pouring 1/3 of a bag of sugar over figs (do not add water) once figs are in the Dutch oven turn stove on high for 1 hour until figs begin to bubble. Once figs begin to bubble turn figs down to 6 or medium high. Cook for additional 1 ½ hour. OPTIONAL: put sugar on figs then leave figs in the pot over night. Then cook for 1 ½ hours.

Note: I remember when my mom was picking figs on my Uncle Olan and Aunt Mammie's fig tree. All of a sudden my mom screamed and said there was a snake on the tree. My uncle snatched the rattler by the tail and whirled the rattler round and round until he snapped his wrist and snapped the head of the snake off. Needless to say, she was always cautious picking figs from then on.

Deborah Odom

Chicken Cream Sauce

3 cups of chicken stock

salt

6 TBSP chicken fat or butter

pepper

6 TBSP sifted all purpose flour

1 TBSP parsley flakes

Make a roux by cooking the fat or butter and flour in the top of a double boiler. Cook for 5 minutes. Add hot chicken stock and stir to prevent lumping. Season with salt and pepper. Add parsley

Chicken Wraps

- 3 chicken breast with skin on
- 1 c. medium dried celery stalk
- olive oil
- 1/4 c. scallions chopped
- kosher salt
- 1/4 c. golden raisins
- grd. black pepper
- 1 c. salted cashews, pecans or peanuts
- 3 minced garlic cloves chopped
- 1 c. grated mozzarella cheese
- 6 tortillas
- 1 tsp. curry powder
- 1/2 c. mayonnaise
- 1/2 cup of mango, peach or apricot chutney

Pre heat oven to 350° place washed and dried chicken breasts on a sheet pan and rub skin with olive oil. Sprinkle liberally with salt and pepper. Rub 1 minced garlic clove under each chicken skin. Roast for 35 to 40 minutes. Let chicken rest. De bone, remove skin and shred chicken pieces

DRESSING: combine mayo chutney, curry powder and ½ tsp salt in food processor and pulse until smooth Combine chicken dressing celery, raisins, scallions and nuts, blend well and refrigerate for a few hours. In tortilla wrap place lettuce leaves and sprinkle mozzarella cheese Spoon chicken mixture and roll up. Slice diagonally and serve with apple slices and grapes.

Child Play Dough (Not To Be Eaten)

1 cup flour

2 tsp. cream tartar

1/2 cup salt

Food Coloring

1 cup water

Flavoring

1 TBSP cooking oil

Combine all ingredients in a saucepan. A flavoring such as peppermint, oil of wintergreen, or banana oil may be added. Cook until soft. Drop onto waxed paper and knead to remove lumps. Store in an airtight container.

Note: Children enjoy this product better than the commercial product. It is hard to decide if it is the product or the memory of making the product that they enjoy the most.

Children's Hand Candles

Bunches of white sand

Several wicks

Some melted paraffin

A variety of citrus oils

Fill a flat aluminum pie pan with dampened white sand. Let the child press their hand well into the sand leaving a hand print. Smooth around it and pour melted paraffin and scent over a small wick. Let stand for an hour.

Note: Great for rainy days or at a beach or park picnic.

Decorative Baskets & Ornaments

1 cup salt

1 1/4 cups water

4 cups flour

Mix ingredients and knead about 20 minutes, or until of desired consistency. Dough can be used in any creative way. Baskets may be made by weaving dough on back side of Pyrex baking dish. To make ornaments, roll dough and cut out shapes with cookie cutters. Prick to prevent air bubbles. Dampen to make pieces stick together. Bake at 300 degrees until golden brown. Paint with acrylic paints. Let dry and varnish.

Finger Paints

3 TBSP sugar

liquid detergent

1/2 c. cornstarch

saucepan

2 c. cold water

4 to 5 small jars

food coloring

Mix the sugar and cornstarch then add the water. Cook over heat stirring constantly until well blended. Divide the mixture in 4 to 5 jars and add a different food color to each. Add a pinch of detergent for easy clean up.

Fricassee Sauce

3 TBSP butter

1/2 c. cream

4 TBSP all purpose flour

1/8 tsp. garlic powder

2 c. chicken stock

1 tsp. black or white pepper

Melt butter add flour cook until bubbly. Add chicken stock and cook until smooth. Stirring constantly. Add cream and continue cooking until thickened and smooth. Season to your taste.

House Seasoning:

1 cup salt

1/4 cup garlic powder

1/4 cup black pepper

1/4 cup dried parsely flakes

Mix ingredients together and store in an airtight container for up to 6 months.

Kool-Aid Clay

2 pkgs. unsweetened kool-aid   1/2 c. salt

2 c. boiling water   saucepan

1 TBSP cream of tartar   2 1/2 c. flour mixing bowl

3 TBSP oil

Mix together dry ingredients. Add water and oil, mix thoroughly, let cool, and store in an airtight container.

Let It Snow

2 cups Ivory Snow   1 cup Water

Put 2 cups of Ivory Snow and 1 cup of water in a large mixing bowl. Beat on high speed adding water if necessary until mixture is light and fluff.

Note: This can also be used to decorate Christmas trees, greenery, or pinecones and will last indefinitely after applied.

Deborah Odom

Mayonnaise

2 eggs whole

1 TBSP lemon juice

1/4 tps dry mustard

1/2 tsp. salt

1/4 paprika

1 c. salad oil

Blend all ingredients except oil at high speed. Turn blender on low speed & add steady stream of oil slowly. Blend for a few seconds or until mayo consistency.

Mouth Watering Pecans

2 TBSP butter, melted

1/4 tsp. salt

2 TBSP light corn syrup

4 c. (about 1 pound) pecan halves

2 tsp. sugar

Stir together butter, salt, corn syrup, and sugar. Add pecans, tossing to coat. Spread coated nuts in a single layer on a larger jellyroll pan. Bake for 1 hour stirring every 15 minutes. Let cool; store in an airtight container for up to 2 weeks.

Open Faced Tuna Sandwhich

1 can tuna in water drained

salt & paprika (for taste)

3 1/2 oz. mayonnaise

4 pieces of white bread

(3-oz.) heavy cream

2 1/2 oz. grated cheese

1/2 lemon juice

2 egg whites

Mix mayonnaise, lemon juice, salt and paprika with the tuna meat. Fold in the whipped cream. Toast the bread, and divide the tuna meat on the 4 slices. The oven should be about 425 degrees. However, the next step makes it even better, so whip the egg whites stiff, fold in the cheese, and pile it on the tuna meat and put in the warm oven for about 5 minutes. Watch it that it does not get too much heat. OPTIONAL: Add white sauce.

Note: You can use crab meat, shrimp or salmon in place of the tuna.

Recipe For A Happy Home

1/2 c. friendship

pinch tenderness

1 c. thoughtfulness

1 bowl of loyalty

1 c. of Faith

1 c. of Hope

1 c. of Charity

1 TBSP of Gaiety

A heaping TBSP of laughter as needed and teaspoons of sympathy

Add a cup of thoughtfulness cream together with a pinch of powdered tenderness very lightly beaten in a bowl of loyalty with a cup of faith one of hope and one of charity be sure to add a spoonful each of gaiety that sings and also the ability to laugh at little things. Moisten with the sudden tears of heartfelt sympathy Bake in good natured pan and serve repeatedly.

Seasoning In A Pinch

4 oz. garlic salt

2 tsp. fresh black ground pepper

4 oz. onion salt

2 TBSP paprika

4 oz. celery salt

1 TBSP chili powder

1 tsp. cayenne or red pepper

1 TBSP sugar

Mix together by sifting three times. Store in a tight container and do not put in direct light. This mixture is good on meats, vegetables and in casseroles.

Silly Putty

white glue

food coloring

Sta-Flo Liquid starch

Air tight container

(If you use Elmer's school glue instead of regular white glue, it won't bounce or pick up pictures) Mix 2 parts glue to 1 part liquid starch. Let dry a bit so that it becomes workable. You can add a few drops of food coloring to give the putty some color.

Store in airtight container.

Stain Remover

1 TBSP white vinegar

1 TBSP water softener

1 TBSP salt

To remove climatic stains combine with 1 pint of warm water. Dip up and down. Rinse well and launder. To prevent climatic stains and brown creases, air in sunlight frequently, and fold in new creases.

Deborah Odom

Vegetarian Open Faced Sandwich

1 thinly sliced red onion

1 TBSP chopped pimento

1/2 lb. sharp cheese

1/2 fresh peeled chopped tomato

1 cup canned red kidney beans drained

whole wheat, seedless rye or white bread

Heat oven to 425 degrees F. Butter slices of bread and put into the oven until light, dry and crispy but not brown. Usually, its about 10 to 15 minutes. Saute onion in butter, add cheese, and cook until cheese is melted. Add the beans and pimento. Then you add tomatoes and season with salt and pepper. Put sauteed ingredients on toast.

LaVergne, TN USA
26 February 2011
218034LV00002B/8/A